D0176738

Noah Webster
Master of Words

One American seldom receives the attention he rightly deserves. Noah Webster, Jr., does not often come immediately to mind when one considers those who helped the United States during its infancy. He should. His services were many and unique in the earliest stages of America.

Even as a boy, Noah was fascinated with language and education. He was troubled by the lack of interest shown by others in formal schooling, and the lack of books and proper facilities bothered him even more.

When the fires of the Revolution broke out in the early 1770's, Noah was a student at Yale. Young and impressionable, he was singed by the flames of patriotism. He longed for a chance to join liberty's cause. He wrote down his thoughts about freedom and government, sharing them with leaders who would put together the United States Constitution. Many of his ideas were incorporated into the document.

But more than a spokesman for democratic government, Noah Webster was a champion for youth and education. He knew what books needed to be written, wrote them, and fought for their acceptance within the school framework. Throughout his adult life, he saw the need for developing the mind while enriching the soul.

"A man should set goals which would please God and assist his fellow man," observed Noah Webster, Jr.

Surely, Noah took his own advice. As a boy growing up, he turned to the Bible as his code of behavior and his core of learning. It is not surprising that one of Webster's final literary contributions, and in his opinion, his "most glorious achievement," was his own wording of the King James Bible.

Today, Webster is with us still. But he merits a place of honor beyond a name stamped on dictionaries around the world. He was a man who served his fellow man and his country with unselfish devotion. More importantly, he served his God with faith and love.

Noah Webster

Master of Words

by

David Collins

illustrated by

Michael Denman

Fenton, Michigan 48430

Dedicated to the memory of George Mott,
whose love of God, children and words
was not unlike that of Noah Webster, Jr.

All Scriptures are from the King James Version of the Bible

COPYRIGHT © 1989 by Mott Media

All rights in this book are reserved. No portion of this book may be reproduced by any process such as mimeograph, photocopying, recording, storage in a retrieval or transmitted by any means without written permission of the publisher. Brief quotations embodied in critical articles or reviews are permitted. For information write Mott Media, 112 East Ellen, Fenton, Michigan 48430.

Kurt Dietsch, Cover Artist

LIBRARY OF CONGRESS CATALOGING IN PUBLICATION DATA

Collins, David R.
   Noah Webster: Master of Words / by David Collins.

   p.   cm.—(Sowers Series)
   Bibliography: p. 147
   Includes index.

   SUMMARY: A biography of the teacher who authored the first dictionary written in the United States.
   ISBN 0-88062-158-3
   1. Webster, Noah, 1758-1843—Juvenile literature.
2. Lexicographers—United States—Biography—Juvenile literature.
3. Educators—United States—Biography—Juvenile literature.
[1. Webster, Noah, 1758-1843.   2. Lexicographers. 3. Teachers.]
I. Title. II. Series: Sowers.
PE64.W5C65   1989   423'.092'4—dc19 [B] [92]   89-3095
                                                     CIP AC

ISBN 0-88062-158-3   Paperbound

CONTENTS

1

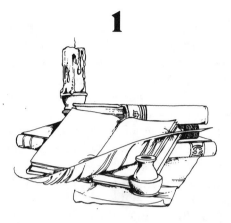

Tragedy In Hartford

Something was wrong.

Reaching the ridge of the Connecticut hillside, seven-year-old Noah Webster quickened his step. He did not pause to look eastward and take in the view of Hartford as he usually did. On this particular afternoon in the year of our Lord, 1766, something else captured the boy's thoughts. It caused the boy to shiver and break into a quick run. Just ahead, near the entry to the Webster's white house, Old Isaiah stood nervously scratching the soil at the front stoop. The horse was untied, a rare sight indeed, but even more strange was the fact that he was there at all. It meant Noah's father was home. Yes, something was wrong.

"Mother!" Noah shouted, flinging open the wooden door. "Why is Father home?"

The boy's shout met only a chorus of whispers, the eerie sounds of the brisk May winds slipping between the pine boards of the two-story structure. Quickly Noah hurried to the stone chimney located in the center of the building. It was there he found his mother each day after school, tending food over the brick oven. Today was no exception. But seldom had Noah seen his mother wear such a troubled face.

Mercy Steele Webster was known by her friends and neighbors as a woman of kindness and energy. A great-granddaughter of the Plymouth Colony governor William Bradford, Mercy was quite content to stand in her husband's shadow, providing her children with a hearty amount of God's love and a spotless home as well.

"Do you always enter the house shouting so?"

The sound of his father's stern voice startled Noah. The older man appeared at the open doorway across the room. His face, too, was more solemn than usual, drained of the ruddy glow that each man and boy of the Webster family always displayed.

Like his wife, Noah Webster, Sr., enjoyed a respected reputation among the people of West Hartford and the neighboring community. A lieutenant during the French and Indian Wars, he had returned from battle to farm some eighty acres of rich Yankee soil. Since their marriage on January 12, 1749, Noah Webster, Sr., and his wife Mercy had been blessed with five healthy babies—Mercy, born November 8, 1749; Abraham, born September 17, 1751; Jerusha, born January 22, 1756; Noah, Jr., born October 16, 1758; and Charles, born September 2, 1762.

"I--I am sorry, Father," young Noah offered, moving silently to his mother's side as she slowly stirred the stew she was cooking in an open iron pot in the oven. "You are never home at this time. I was afraid---"

"Fear can be the devil's playmate," Master Webster countered. "The only fear you might have now is that of not completing your chores before dinner."

With his head bowed, Noah turned away, but his curiosity caused him to turn back before leaving the room. "Yet *you* are here, Father, and you are never home this early. Is there a reason?"

Master Webster glanced at his wife. "The boy asks more questions than all the rest of them together. Surely the Lord has sent him here to test our patience."

Mercy Webster allowed a sliver of a smile to cross her lips as she lifted a wooden spoon from the pot. "The boy is only seven," the woman said softly. "Would you have him be curious. . .or ignorant?" She extended the spoon, drawing her husband forward to sample the taste of her stew.

"To your chores, lad," said his father, as he turned and faced him. "I shall answer your questions at mealtime so that I should not have to tell each of you separately."

His father's words did little to quell young Noah's curiosity, but the boy knew well his father's tone of voice. For the present, the matter was ended. It would be discussed at mealtime.

There were always chores to do around the Webster home. The scattered farms that dotted the Connecticut countryside each boasted their own pastures, meadows and stone walls. There were cows to milk and graze, tools to mend and sharpen, corn to hoe and pick, hay to cut, potatoes to dig, kindling to chop—the list was long and tiring. What amusement there was fell to one's own resourcefulness. A nearby woods invited youthful explorers, while its pond offered fishing in the summertime and skating during the winter. Cornhusking time provided a chance to gather together and exchange conversation while shucking kernels into barrels.

But it was the schoolhouse that gave seven-year-old

Noah Webster the greatest joy. Younger boys and girls attended classes during the spring and summer, even into autumn, while the older children went in the winter when they were not needed for plowing, planting and harvesting. Most of the school lessons came from the Bible, a Primer, and the Thomas Dilworth Speller. With care and caution, Noah and his classmates filled manuscript booklets with their goose-penned letters and figures. A waxed rod awaited the palms and posteriors of those students who did not take quickly enough to the schoolmaster's dictated lessons. Students recited aloud, and were evaluated more on volume and enunciation than on understanding of content.

But if young Noah Webster failed to learn at school, there were other opportunities. Noah Webster, Sr., was a church deacon who insisted on daily Bible readings at home, blessings before each meal and regular gathering of the family for prayer. Sunday afternoons afforded a chance to discuss the two-hour sermon heard that morning at the West Hartford Congregational Church. "You may lose your way traveling through Connecticut," Master Webster told his children, "but in this home, you will always know the pathway to the Lord."

On this particular May afternoon, Noah Webster, Jr., cared little about any pathway at all. All he wanted to know was why his father was home so early. Surely Abram would know, Noah thought. His fourteen-year-old brother seemed to know everything. A quick search found the older boy hoeing in the corn fields.

"Father is home!" Noah exclaimed. "Did you see him?"

Abram glanced up, but his muscular arms did not miss a movement as they sent the hoe biting into the soil. "Yes, I saw him ride to the house some time ago."

"But why is he home? Did you not run to ask?"

Abram shook his head, his movements still in paced rhythm to his work. "Should he wish me to know, he would tell me," the boy answered.

"But-but--" It was useless to say anything else, and Noah knew it. Such matters did not trouble Abram. Noah turned, wondering where his sisters might be. Moments later he found them outside the back door. They chattered quietly as they worked as a team to churn butter. Ten-year-old Jerusha glanced up.

"And how did young Master Webster perform at school today?" she asked. "Did he stump the schoolmaster with a new word from the *Connecticut Courant*?" The *Courant* was the weekly newspaper that entered the Webster home, consumed and discussed largely by young Noah and his father.

"I need no teasing," Noah declared. "I need to know why Father is home."

Mercy stopped turning the tired wooden crank on the churn. She looked up, her face showing confusion. "He rode home a while ago, jumped off of Old Isaiah, and raced into the house. We were helping Mother quilt, but he sent us out here."

"Why don't you ask him?" Rusha asked, her voice still cradled in a teasing lilt. "I am certain he would tell *you*."

Noah shook his head. "I did ask, but he would tell me nothing. He sent me to do my chores.."

"And is talking to us one of them?" Rusha queried, her eyes stealing a glance at her older sister. "I am sure not."

Annoyance flashed in young Noah's brown eyes as he turned. His jaw jutted defiantly, his ruddy cheeks matching the redness of his tousled hair. No one ever seemed to have the answers he wanted. Worse yet, no one else seemed to care. It was the same way at school. He could lose himself quickly in his reading and writing, while others idly wasted their time, cutting the wooden benches and tables with pen knives or carrying on some foolish pin lottery. No one wished to be bothered with questions, whether they were about the lesson being studied or any other topic. At seven, Noah spent much of the year at the schoolhouse. But soon, he would attend only in the winter, like his older brothers and sisters.

Slowly, the boy retraced his steps to join Abram in the corn fields. Perhaps hoeing would make him forget about the mystery concerning his father.

Despite his efforts, Noah could not shove the question from his mind. He was grateful when the family was finally seated around the dinner table. He could hardly wait until his father had finished the blessing, but on this night there was an extra prayer.

". . .and may our loving God find a special place in Paradise for the six young souls of Hartford who have left their home on earth this day. Amen."

As Master Webster stopped speaking, Noah looked up to meet the equally surprised looks of his two sisters across the table. Abram, too, looked shocked, while four-year-old Charles wore his usual expression as he awaited his mother's help with his food. Mrs. Webster complied, silently.

Noah could not contain himself another moment. "Father, who are the six young souls of Hartford? Is that why you were home early today from the fields?"

Master Webster nodded, his face grim. "There was an explosion today at the Hartford schoolhouse. The stove overheated. Six of the children were killed.

Again, Noah glanced at Mercy, Rusha and Abram. None could find words to speak. They were grimly contemplating that the tragedy could have happened in their schoolhouse at West Hartford.

"We are going to look at the West Hartford schoolhouse before you return, Noah. We have known the roofs of the schoolhouses are leaky, and the walls too thin. But we did not expect anything like this would happen." Master Webster gazed at his wife. "We shall be visiting the families of the children."

Mrs. Webster turned her attention from Charles. "We will prepare some food baskets, daughters." Mercy and Jerusha nodded.

But something still disturbed seven-year-old Noah. Thoughts leaped around in his mind as he tried to recall the preacher's words not long ago. There was something out of place, something too confusing. The boy sat forward.

"But when Mrs. Jessup was crying," Noah said, "when her mother died, remember what the preacher said? He said it is nature's law that children must bury their parents. Do you remember that? I remember it."

Master Webster nodded, and young Noah turned to see his mother nod too.

"But what is this, Father?" the boy continued. "Is it also nature's law that parents bury their children?" Noah knew he was questioning again, but he wanted to know, to have an answer.

For several moments Master Webster did not speak. No one else did either. Even Charles seemed to sense the mood at the table and said nothing. Finally, Noah Webster, Sr., rose and went to the nearby fireplace. His solemn face captured a golden hue from the coals and embers.

"No, it is not nature's law that fathers and mothers bury their children." The man stopped, lifted a long switch and nudged a sparkcrusted log. "Nature's laws are those we understand. Evening's darkness follows the light of day. Summer follows spring. Nature's laws

are fairly simple. It is God's law that is not so easy
to understand, and God's law is above nature's law
and all the rest. We may have questions at times, but
we must have faith that God is loving and knows all
the answers. We may learn some of those answers
while we are on this earth, but others we will learn
when we are finally with Him.''

Noah, Jr., did not eat as much that evening as he
usually did. Nor did sleep come quickly. The boy
thought and prayed for the six children of Hartford.
And he also thanked God for providing him with a
father who wore a stern face, spoke with a firm voice,
but who had a patient and loving heart.

2

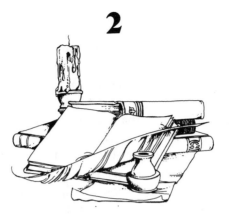

The Smell Of Love

By the time Noah Jr. was ten, each weekly issue of the *Connecticut Courant* was more dismal than the issue before it. Now and then the newspaper was hurled into the fire before the boy had an opportunity to read it.

"It is not worth the time," Master Webster declared, shaking his head in disgust. "Only more news of the injustices we suffer from those thieves in England."

"Injustices?" Noah asked, always eager to learn a new word. "What are 'injustices'? Who are the thieves in England?"

"The injustices are the taxes and tariffs that are placed on everything we buy from the old country. The thieves are those greedy representatives in Parliament who would make us pay for every breath we take, if they could. Tariffs on coffee, taxes on molasses, and we have no voice in the matter."

"Then I say we do not pay," Noah Jr. answered firmly. "If the taxes are unfair, we should not have to pay them."

"And will you tell that to the soldiers they send?"
his father asked. "Each ship from England brings
more of the red lobsterbacks. It will come to a bad
end, I am thinking...a bad end indeed."

But if the weekly *Courant* brought gloom and anger
to the Webster house, the *Ames Almanack* brought an-
ticipation and good cheer. Published each year, the
booklet contained a full calendar with notes about the
weather, a collection of bright poems and maxims, as
well as articles about animals, plants and foods.
It was a welcome addition to every New England
home each December, and the members of the
Webster family read it cover to cover.

It was one issue of the *Ames Almanack* that put
Abram, Noah Jr. and Charles into whole-hearted
competition. Master Webster discovered an article
about growing roses on one of the almanack pages,
and suggested his three sons each attempt to raise a
bush of his own.

"I shall talk to Hezekiah Merrill in the town,"
Master Webster said. "He sometimes has hearty
sprouts for planting. Then we shall see which of you
can grow the handsomest shrub."

"Where shall we plant our rose bushes, Father?"
inquired seventeen-year-old Abram. "There is hardly
an open space on the entire farm."

Sensing his son was not overjoyed about another
task, Master Webster smiled. "I know of just the spot
on the far side of the orchard."

"But why so far away from the house?" asked
Charles.

"So that your mother will not see them," came the
answer. "I think fresh roses for your mother's
birthday might bring a special joy to her spirit and
a smile to her face. Especially coming from her favorite

young lads. The girls are crocheting her a shawl.''

Noah, Jr. had been unusually silent. He had read the article about roses but had thought little about it. As far as Hezekiah Merrill's store was concerned, the only thing that interested him was the fine collection of small books he kept displayed. Whenever Noah accompanied his father or mother to the mercantile south of the Hartford Courthouse, the boy enjoyed reading while his parents purchased needed wares. But if his father said there were rose sprouts or plants, Noah did not doubt it for a moment. Not only that, the thought of a contest among his brothers excited him. It would mean little to do something— anything—better than Charles. After all, he was three years younger. But bettering Abram—now that was worth the effort.

''When can we get started, Father?'' Noah, Jr., asked.

The next time the Webster wagon rolled into Hartford to visit the store of Hezekiah Merrill, young Noah stayed beside his father. He listened and watched as his father bought supplies, then happily selected the three small rose shoots himself. Before the men left, Master Merrill led young Noah to a side counter.

''Perhaps your blooms will be as this one,'' the storeowner said, holding his hand in a cup. Inside rested a lifelike deep red rose made of velvet. ''It looks almost real, doesn't it? The ladies of the court of King George are said to favor such blossoms on their dresses.''

Noah's eyes widened in amazement. How real the petals looked, as if they had just this moment come from the sunlight. Master Merrill held the flower to his nose.

''Why, I believe I can even smell the fragrance,''

the storeowner offered, winking at the boy.

Noah glanced at his father, and all three of them laughed. But in his laughter, the boy promised that he would do everything possible to grow the best roses for his mother.

As soon as he reached home, Noah Jr. hurried to the spot near the orchard where his father had told them they could plant their bushes. He had read the article over and over, learning how to ready the soil, how to handle the plant, how much water and sunlight were needed—every detail. It took him only a few minutes to clear the spot and plant his shoot. He knew it would be just as easy to clear a space for Charles' plant—and Abram's too. But why should he, Noah asked himself. Perhaps Charles would forget to plant his. His younger brother was always forgetting something. As for Abram, perhaps he would be too tired from his chores that day. "The sooner the plant makes a home within the soil, the better possibilities for its hale and hearty growth." So read the article in the almanack. Therefore Noah carefully planted his own rose plant that afternoon, then went cheerfully to his other chores.

It was not until the next day that Abram planted his small rose bush, and the day after that for Charles. Already Noah thought his handsome plant had taken root and begun its quest for life. Each morning he visited the rosebush before he started his daily chores. How bright the tiny specks of dew sparkled on the leaves that appeared. They were like the glittering lights of the sky at night. He could not resist smiling as he looked over at Abram's rosebush several feet away. It seemed to spread sideways, twisted and gnarled in every direction. And Charles' crude bush seemed to suddenly surround itself with weeds. Noah's first impulse was to pull the weeds himself, keeping his younger brother's as free from any possible hindrances as his own. But something stopped him from such an urge. Instead, he promised to tell Charles at supper that his rosebush was engulfed in tiny weeds. Yet when the opportunity presented itself, Noah did not say a word about the situation. He decided to tell Charles what to do if his younger brother asked— after all, wasn't it Charles' responsibility to take care of his own rosebush? Seven years old was quite old enough for such a task, Noah reasoned, and if the weeds killed the rosebush, it was Charles' own fault!

It was not long before both Mercy and Jerusha sensed there was something going on among their brothers that the two girls knew nothing about. Although most of the girls' chores kept them near the house, they caught bits and pieces of conversation they did not understand.

"You should have told me about those weeds," Charles scolded Noah one night after supper. "They could have killed it, if Abram had not told me."

"Could have killed *what?*" Jerusha immediately wanted to know. "What are you talking about?"

Noah shook his head at his brother. "You should have read the almanack too," he answered. "I'm not going to do everything for you all the time."

"I believe Jerusha asked you a question, dear brother." This time it was Mercy who joined the discussion. "And I am just as interested as she is. What weeds are you talking about? Why are weeds so important all of a sudden?"

Clearly, Noah had heard his sister's question. But he had no intention of offering answers. He hurried to the door and cupped one hand around his ear. "My, that wind blows heavy and hot this evening. Why, it even sounds a bit like my two sisters, Mercy and Jerusha. No, that couldn't be. They would not be talking so much about matters that do not concern them.''

Mercy and Jerusha exchanged knowing looks. It was not the first time the Webster boys had shut them out of their conversation. But they, too, were not without their own weapons.

"Mother," Mercy asked. "If Jerusha and I pick extra berries, may we bake a pie all of our own, to do with whatever we please?''

Mrs. Webster sat darning near the fire. It was her favorite place after the meal was completed, the table cleared, and before thoughts turned to going to bed. She glanced up at Mercy's question. ''I would not be one to say no when my children offer to do more than their share of their duties. Goodness knows, it is enough work to get that much done. But baking an extra pie? That sounds noble enough...but I sense you have little thought of sharing with everyone.''

"Oh, we will share with you, Mother," Mercy promised. "Won't we, Jerusha?''

Jerusha nodded. ''And Father too,'' the younger girl added.

"Oh, yes," Mercy agreed. ''We will save a big piece for Father. But I think this pie will have but four pieces in it, unlike those we usually serve.''

Noah's face reddened. It always did when he angered. "Listen to her, Father. I believe she needs reminding of the Good Book, where it tells us to share the gifts the Lord provides...''

This time it was Jerusha who reddened. ''Oh, so it is good enough for you boys to keep secrets among yourselves, but if we choose not to share, then it is against the teachings of the Lord, Well, good brother of mine, reflect on Psalm 128:2 'Thou shalt eat the labours of thy hands.' And that is just what we intend to do, don't we, Mercy?''

"It certainly is!"

Master Webster moved to a spot behind his wife's chair. He lay one hand gently on her shoulder. "We have raised a lively crop, have we not, woman? Their tongues wag a bit sharp this evening."

Mrs. Webster nodded. "Perhaps an early time to bed would offer extra moments for quiet reflection."

"A wise suggestion."

Not one of the Webster family failed to understand the signal to retire for the night. Fifteen minutes later, the three boys heard a light rap on the door of the upstairs bedroom they shared. Master Webster entered, carrying a candle. He seated himself in the sole wooden chair.

"I would not like to think the rosebushes you are growing for your mother will cause a family feud." Master Webster offered softly.

Noah raised himself up in bed. "Those girls are always meddling, Father. I, for one, want none of their silly pies. Jerusha always burns the crust anyway."

"Enough of that, boy. I did not come in here tonight to talk of such matters. I am wondering if perhaps it might not be wise to share what you are doing with your sisters. The surprise, after all, is for your mother."

"But if Mercy and Rusha know, they will surely tell Mother," Abram declared. "Their tongues are never still."

Master Webster rubbed his chin. "It *is* true that they are not the quietest children in these parts..."

"In ANY parts!" Noah blurted out. The boy slipped lower under the coverlet when he saw his father's disapproving glance.

"Well, it should not be much longer before the roses will be in bloom. You may, however, have to do without a piece or two of berry pie.''

"It is a small sacrifice in exchange for our our sisters' silence,'' murmured Abram.

"True enough!'' Noah agreed.

Quietly Master Webster rose, still carrying the flickering candle, and moved toward the door. "The secret shall remain,'' he said, "but I want your promise that you will remember your sisters kindly in your prayers.''

"Can we just promise to remember our sisters?'' Noah whispered across the room, his voice teasing.

"The word is 'kindly' I say. Now, may the Lord bless your sleep.''

With that, Master Webster was gone. Noah snuggled under the coverlet. "Abram, do you suppose Mother is talking with Mercy and Jerusha?'' Noah asked.

"Sh-h-h!'' Abram answered.

It was but a few minutes later that Noah heard the sound of a door open and close across the hall. Mother returned downstairs.

Little more was said about the rosebushes in the Webster house. It seemed clear enough that Mercy and Jerusha had been told not to investigate matters that were not their own. As for the berry pies, the boys and girls of the Webster family shared evenly without the slightest confrontation. In truth, Noah thought the pies were the best the girls had ever prepared, but he refrained from making such an observation for fear of being misunderstood.

Inch by inch, the rosebushes grew. The article in *Ames Almanack* suggested adding a support trellis or fence behind any bush of substantial growth. Although Noah's hardly qualified for such a definition, Noah carefully pieced one together anyway, from kindling scraps, and placed it behind the bush. There was no doubt whose bush reigned supreme. Abram's still continued to spread from side to side, while Charles' boasted few buds on rather spindly branches. Only Noah's looked anything like the drawing in the almanack.

A week before the birthday, the buds suddenly burst into bloom. Noah could hardly control his joy. He wanted to pick the soft, red blossoms and hurry them to the house. But that would ruin the surprise. Anyway, seven days and the flowers would be even more impressive. He chuckled at the tiny blossoms on Abram's bush. Charles', too, were small and sickly. But Noah's were perfect, all three of them like the velvet cloth rose in Master Merrill's store.

Six days.

Five.

Four.

Every morning Noah arose earlier, eager to hurry and see his rosebush. He loved the sight of the sparkling dewdrops on the red petals. Each morning another bud popped open, stretching toward the warm sunrays. Noah coaxed his father to the sight one day, and the boy sensed the older man's pride as well as his own. "I'm only sorry Abram and Charles did not fare as well with their bushes," Master Webster said. Noah nodded, but did not speak. In truth, he felt little sorrow for his brothers. After all, he had worked harder. Why shouldn't he get the greatest satisfaction?

And then it happened—only two days before Mrs. Webster's birthday. All night the thunder rolled across the Connecticut countryside, with jagged strips of lightning snapping across the sky. Rain pounded the Webster roof hour after hour. Early morning chores were postponed until the weather calmed. Finally, Master Webster headed out to the barn even though the downpour continued. The cow could not wait to be milked, after all.

There were always tasks to do inside, and Mrs.
Webster seemed never to tire of assigning them. But
she, too, seemed relieved when Master Webster
returned to the house. He wore a sad look.

"The storm has damaged some of the crops and
orchards. I'm afraid..."

Before his father had finished, Noah was into his
coat and running out the door. The rosebush! All he
could think about was the rosebush. He ran all the
way to the spot.

There it was—a beaten and battered mess. The
storm had destroyed the once proud bush, leaving only
a tangled mound of vine and leaves. Abram's and
Charles' bushes were equally ruined. No bud or
blossom remained in the mud. "Why?" Noah
whispered to the damp morning air. "It was for
Mother..."

The rest of the day was spent trying to clean up
around the Webster house and farm. Few words were
spoken. By dinnertime, Noah knew both Abram and
Charlie had seen the ravaged rosebushes. It was in
their sad eyes.

And tomorrow was Mother's birthday. Before Noah
went to bed, he counted the few coins he had saved
in his wooden box under his bed. He had hoped to
buy one of the books Master Merrill sometimes
displayed at his store. If only he had saved more, he
thought. Then he could at least give his mother a
handful of coins. But there were only four half
pennies...

"I'll be going to Merrill's Store very early in the
morning," Master Webster told his sons at bedtime.
"We need wire and nails for repair. I'll need to take
one of you. The other two can stay here and work
around the barn. We'll try to salvage what we can
in the orchard."

Noah did not sleep well that night. All he could think about was his rosebush. The more he thought about it, the more convinced he was that the storm was a punishment. At first he had wanted to have the best roses for his mother so she would be happy. But then it had become an effort to show up his two brothers. It was the Lord's way of showing displeasure—Noah was sure of it.

But by the next morning, he was ready to go with his father. Noah took the coins from the box. When his father asked him if he had enough for one of Master Merrill's books, Noah nodded. Yet when they arrived at the store, Noah went nowhere near the shelf that held the books. He had something else to buy. His father just smiled.

It was not until that evening that Noah revealed the surprise gift he had purchased at Merrill's Store. By the light of the fire, Mrs. Webster pulled away the paper that lay wrapped around one red velvet rose. "Why, Noah," the woman exclaimed, holding the cloth flower so all could see. "It's lovely..."

"Oh, Mother, may I hold it for a moment?" Jerusha asked. "I have never seen anything so beautiful."

"Neither have I," her older sister said.

Noah enjoyed seeing his mother's smiling face and hearing her happy voice. There had been little laughter in the house on this birthday. It was good to hear his sisters' joy too.

Abram leaned forward from his chair in the kitchen where he was whittling, Charlie glanced up as he sat on the hearth. He had just opened his mouth to speak when Noah walked to his Mother's chair.

"It's from all of us boys," Noah said, shooting a look first at Charles and then at Abram. "We knew Mercy and Jerusha were crocheting you a shawl.

Perhaps you can pin this on it.''

Master Webster gazed at his middle son with new admiration and respect. Abram shared a similar look, while Charles was still too stunned to say anything.

Mrs. Webster pulled her new shawl around her shoulders. ''Oh, I shall wear it here,'' she said, placing the flower at her neck. I have no brooches, as some women have, but this shall look even better.''

Noah looked down. ''I-I only wish it smelled like a real rose...''

Mrs. Webster looked at the velvet flower, then held it to her nose and sniffed. ''Why, I can smell it. Umm-...yes, indeed, I can.''

Noah was puzzled. A cloth flower that smelled? He bent lower and sniffed. No, there was no smell at all. ''I can't smell anything, Mother.''

Again Mrs. Webster held the rose to her face. ''Oh, yes, my son. This rose smells of love...and that is the most beautiful smell in the world.''

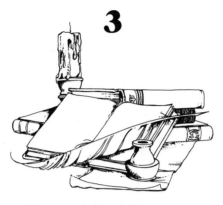

3

The Road
To Wisdom

Carefully, Noah Webster sprinkled the black powder into the wooden bowl and stirred. The soot dissolved with the vinegar, the mashed and boiled walnut hulls, and the salt.

"What are you making, Noey?" Charlie asked.

"It's ink."

Charlie edged closer, hovering over his older brother's shoulder. "It's black, not brown. Did the schoolmaster say we had to write with black ink?"

Noah did not want to be bothered. "It is not for the schooomaster," he snapped. "Brown ink is fine for the schoolmaster. Now can you not find something else to do?"

Charlie would not be put off. "You always used brown ink before. Why are you making black ink now?"

"Must you ask so many questions, Charlie?"

From behind the pages of the *Connecticut Courant* near the fireplace came a muffled cough. Master Webster set the newspaper in his lap as he rested in his

armchair. ''How fast the years slip by! Is this my son
Noah who tires so quickly from questioning? It seems
like only yesterday that *he* was the seven-year-old per-
sistent questioner at Abram's arm, or with his sisters,
Mercy and Rusha, wanting to know anything they
learned.''

''It was very little indeed, Father,'' thirteen-year-
old Noah retorted, glancing up from the table. But
the boy understood what his father was saying.

''I am mixing black ink for the Reverend Perkins.
He has said a bit of soot makes for a darker line when
writing. The Reverend learned that at Princeton. He
has asked to see my script so I have decided to mix
black ink as he suggested.''

''What are you going to write?'' Charlie asked.

Noah reached for his favorite goose-quill pen, setting the bowl of ink to the side. On a piece of paper,
he began to write, being careful to form each letter
with the straightness and swirl it demanded.

No Man may put off the Law of God.
The Way of God is no ill Way.
My Joy is in God all the Day.
A bad Man is a Foe to God.

It took the young boy an hour to write the maxims
to his own satisfaction, and Charlie could not endure
the tension and precision of his brother's efforts. By
the time he had finished, Noah looked up to find his
father where his brother had been.

''Your thoughts, lad?'' Master Webster queried.

Noah shook his head as he set the pen down. ''No,
they are from the Dilworth text. But do you know how
amazing they are? Each word is no longer than three
letters.''

His father nodded. ''You and your word games.
I have never seen anyone so taken with words. You

show a clever wit, Noah, with this ability you have with words. Just be certain you think of what is said as well as the cleverness of *how* it is said.''

As his father rose and went off to bed, Noah stared at the words he had written. Yes, each had no more than three letters, but together, strung together like beads on a bracelet, they carried such meaning. Words. They could carry such force, such power. Yet they could bring joy and laughter. Fear, too. And they could convey beauty, of what was seen and what was felt deep inside. Words. How wonderful they were.

If anyone in West Hartford shared young Noah's love for words, it was the new minister. His arrival in April of 1772 had some members of the church parish wagging their tongues. After all, the Reverend Nathan Perkins was fresh out of Princeton. Many of the older parishioners were more than a bit skeptical about the young preacher's worth. ''We'll probably have to be explaining the Bible to the new shaver ourselves,'' was the general consensus. But from his first service, the Reverend made his presence felt without challenge. His knowledge of the Bible was deep and vast, and the lessons to be drawn were clearly explained. No longer did the tongues wag as week after week Preacher Perkins drew the members in, seasoned them with the warmth and flavor of God's love, then sent them out to share a better world with those they met.

At thirteen, Noah Webster, Jr. was perhaps too young to capture all that he heard from the minister of the West Hartford Congregational Parish, but he knew he loved listening. In the past, Noah had listened to stories of Cain and Abel, of Moses, of David and Goliath, yes, and even the story of Noah and his ark. Yet, that is all they had seemed—stories. But Reverend Perkins brought the Bible characters to life, made them seem real, showed how they made human mistakes and grew into strong Christians by loving God and His Son, Jesus. From stories, they became truth. Faith lived in Noah's soul and mind. With that living faith there came a growing admiration for Reverend Nathan Perkins. Noah longed to be able to speak like the preacher, with every thought and phrase so perfectly tied together. Yes, the preacher shared the love for language Noah felt. That much was certain.

What was equally certain was that Reverend Perkins sensed young Noah's feelings. No one sat with more focus and attention and asked more delving questions as Perkins taught Bible lessons; no one listened more closely than Noah Webster, Jr., when home visits were made. If Reverend Perkins was disappointed that no one in the entire congregation chose to make a public profession of his religious devotion, he took some consolation from the youth of the parish who seemed excited about their faith. No one was more enthusiastic than Noah.

Boys seldom remained in school beyond the age of thirteen. At fourteen, they were considered men, ready to take on the duties of farming, like their fathers. A few became blacksmiths, millers, storekeepers or shop owners, carrying on the family business. A very few continued their education at college. When Reverend Perkins suggested such a possibility for Noah, Jr., his father expressed interest—with concern. After all, Abraham was the older son and deserved first priority. But when Abram declined the opportunity, preferring to get into farming instead, Master Webster looked with greater favor upon Noah, Jr., continuing his education.

I would be willing to work with young Noah,'' the Reverend Perkins agreed, ''but I would have to be paid for my services. It would not be fair otherwise.''

Master Webster rubbed his chin. Even with the best of crops, there was little money left over each year. Yet one look at the pleading expression on his son's face and the matter was finished—Noah Webster, Jr., would prepare for entrance into college.

The task involved much more than learning to mix and write with black ink rather than brown. The first book Reverend Perkins gave his new student was a Latin grammar text. Flipping through the pages, Noah's eyes widened. It all looked so terribly complicated.

''No college will take in a student who does not know Latin,'' Reverend Perkins asserted. ''Latin is the language of scholars, of great literature, of science and mathematics. If you think it looks too difficult for you, perhaps---''

''Oh no, it does not look difficult at all,'' Noah answered in faked confidence. ''I was merely wondering if this is all I have to learn for my first lesson.''

Reverend Perkins hid his amused smile. ''I believe the text will provide a hearty first lesson. Return when you have mastered a few of the rules.''

Noah nodded, promising himself that nothing else would occupy his time. He kept the promise in the days that followed, although cows slipped away while he studied, and Charles gobbled up his brother's mealtime desserts in exchange for chopping Noah's share of the kindling.

Slowly, ever so slowly, the Latin became clearer to Noah. He carried the book everywhere he went, flipping it open whenever he had a few extra minutes. Reverend Perkins introduced the willing scholar to other books in his library—to a collection of sermons, to a play by Shakespeare, to an anthology of essays by Alexander Pope. They offered thoughts that stretched Noah's mind, made him reach for new ideas. No longer was it enough to merely read aloud with proper enunciation and volume. Reverend Perkins demanded that Noah analyze what he read and explain it. "Tis education forms the common mind," the preacher said often, quoting Pope, "like as the twig is bent, the tree's inclined." Noah listened, continuing to bend the twig a bit farther. Each day he practiced reading and writing Latin and Greek, "the necessities of any student wishing to enter college," declared Reverend Perkins. Master Webster and his wife delighted in Noah's progress, although his brother, Charlie, sometimes complained.

"Noey's always showing off. I have to listen to the schoolmaster all day and then I come home to another schoolmaster at night. He tells me not to say 'afeard' but 'afraid.' He tells me not to say 'kiver but 'cover.' Well, I say I'm about to kiver Noey's mouth with my fist, whether he's afeard or not!"

Master Webster shook his head, "Perhaps you forget Ephesians 4:32 where the Bible reads, 'Be ye kind one to another...' No, Charlie, we'll have no fighting in this house."

"Thank you, Father," Noah said, with more than a trace of spite in his voice toward his brother.

"But, Noah, I think *you* might remember 1 Corinthians 3:19" said his father. "It says *The wisdom of this world is foolishness to God*.' There is much to be said for learning and knowledge in this world, as long as we remember to live by those lessons given us by the greatest Teacher of all, our loving God."

Noah glanced down. "I shall try to remember, Father. Come, Charlie, perhaps I might help you practice your reading. I promise to restrain myself from too many corrections."

Charlie smiled. "That's a fair contract."

From 1772 through the summer of 1774, Noah continued his contract with Reverend Perkins. When the preacher's duties proved too numerous, Noah attended the Hartford Grammar School. There was not a moment to waste. With the passing years, Mercy, Abraham and Jerusha were married and left home. There were fewer mouths to feed yet more tasks to be divided among those remaining. Noah knew his father would probably have to mortgage the farm to pay the bills for college, and the boy felt it only fair to study as hard as he could.

As the fall of 1774 approached, Noah made final plans to become a freshman at Yale. In his wildest dreams, he could not imagine any place that could hold twenty-five hundred books—but that is exactly what the Yale College Library was said to offer. Yet although sixteen-year-old Noah Webster, Jr. was filled with grand and glorious dreams of the future, dark clouds were beginning to form overhead. On the wind were whispers of war, a terrifying and frightening encounter, that would affect every person in America.

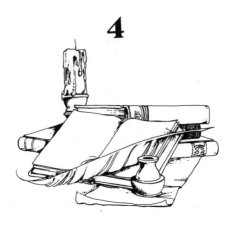

Shadows Of War

For months Noah had anticipated the day when he would finally go off to college. When it arrived, however, his stomach did somersaults and his eyes could not stop clouding. Although Yale College was in New Haven, only thirty-five miles away, the distance seemed much greater. Perhaps it was more the step that was being taken, a step that would take sixteen-year-old Noah away from home for the first time in his life. He was grateful his father was making the journey too, in order to bring back the horse that would carry the boy's belongings, and to pay the bills of enrollment. It was a long hug the departing scholar gave his mother, and although Noah reached for his brother's hand for a hearty handshake, the two boys found themselves in a farewell hug too.

''I shall miss you correcting me,'' Charlie whispered, ''although I would not confess that I learned much from it.''

Noah smiled. "You shall miss my shares of hasty pudding too, for doing my chores when I was study-ing."

"Yes," Charlie laughed, "That too!"

And they were off, Noah, Sr., and Noah, Jr. It was a full day's travel with the boy walking most of the way, his father riding the horse. As soon as he had settled his son in at Connecticut Hall and paid the thirty British pound notes required, Master Webster gave his son the final hug of the day. It was not until later that the boy found a note signed from his father and mother lying on his bed. Once more Noah, Jr., found his eyes clouding as he read:

Our dear young Noah,
We wish to have you serve your generation
and do good in the world and be useful and may
so behave as to gain the esteem of all virtuous
people that are acquainted with you and gain a

*comfortable subsistence, but especially that you
may live so as to obtain the favor of Almighty
God and his grace in this world and a saving
interest in the merits of Jesus Christ, without
which no man can be happy.*

> *Your beloved father and mother*

Noah read the letter over and over until his candle
beside his bed burned low. Finally, he drifted off to
sleep, with a prayer that all within the letter might
come true. He pledged to do all he could to make it so.

There was little beauty in the three structures that
housed Yale College in the fall of 1774. Life for the
150 students, forty of them in Noah's freshman class,
revolved around Connecticut Hall where they studied
and slept; Chapel, which housed a library and
museum in addition to praying facilities; and a
dilapidated blue-colored building which offered
classroom space and a dining hall. The drab
accommodations, as well as the strict rules placed upon
the students, earned Yale the nickname "Brick
Prison" by its resident young scholars.

Two professors, Dr. Naphtali Daggett and Dr.
Nehemiah Strong, reigned supreme in their long black
robes, white wigs and high cocked hats. Daggert, who
was a Doctor of Divinity as well as an expert in all
classical literature, served as president of the school.
Student tutors assisted the two distinguished professors
and more than once Noah blessed Reverend Perkins
for being so demanding in his preparation, as all
classwork was written and recited in Latin.

Not only were the freshmen kept busy with their
assigned lessons in the classroom, the upperclassmen
often had the "fresh bodies" do personal errands.
Boot-greasing was the most common and tedious task,
and it seemed to Noah that he was the freshman asked

most often. "You *are*," one of his classmates confided. "It is because you are always the first to answer the professors. You are always prepared and you seem to know so much."

"I do know," Noah snapped back, "and I will not pretend that I don't. I can grease all the boots in the world, but I will not pretend to be an empty-headed fool."

It was not long before the zealous young freshman found another form of punishment fired in his direction. As he sat in the dining hall eating his boiled meat, turnips and potatoes, he suddenly had the urge to ask Professor Strong a question about the math problem assigned for tomorrow. Noah knew full well that it was improper for students to approach the upper platform where the faculty members took their meals, but he went to Professor Strong anyway. Surprised and annoyed, the instructor sent Noah back to his bench. Before he sat down---

Splat! A juicy piece of meat caught Noah in the middle of his forehead. He looked across the long tables, hoping to catch the culprit. Splat! Another piece of meat hit the back of his head. Noah whirled around, his eyes sparked in anger. But not one face looked suspicious. Everyone kept eating as if nothing had happened. Slowly the boy sat down, no longer having an appetite for eating. However, he had even less appetite for being picked on, and a saying of his father's jumped into his mind and remained. "Vain brings pain," Master Webster had said, and most often it had been directed at Noah. Perhaps, just perhaps, he might have been *too* over-eager to please, too zealous in pursuing answers. Although the boy would never bring himself to deliberately hold back what he knew, he did resolve to be more conscious of others. The resolution seemed to work, for no longer was he the target of meat throwers at dinner.

Latin, Greek, mathematics, philosophy, theology—the daily classroom routine was seldom altered. Not only were the students kept busy with daily recitations, they were required to look after much of their own comforts in the dormitory. They split their own wood, built their own fires and carried in their own water for washing and drinking. The outside privy was tolerable during autumn and spring, but the cold winter nights turned it into a wooden torture box. Disgust with their own facility led a group of upperclassmen to up-end President Daggett's privy one night, a dastardly deed which led to their having to do without metheglin for a week. Metheglin, a tasty concoction of fermented honey and water, was a favorite among the students, but there was general agreement that the deed was well worth the sacrifice.

The daily schedule at the "Brick Prison" seldom varied. On a typical school day, students rose at 5:30 a.m. After dressing, they attended prayers and recitation until 7:30 when they ate breakfast. It was then study time until the bell rang for classes to begin at 11 o'clock. Dinner was promptly at noon, followed by walking and exercising until 3 p.m. There was a three-hour study time until six. Prayer sessions lasted until suppertime, with social recreation following until 9 p.m., when students went to bed.

Sadly, Noah found the Yale Library was not all that he had hoped. True, there were 2500 volumes, but many were beyond reading or totally unrelated to course work. A confused collection of motheaten stuffed birds and animals passed as a museum. The treeless common on which the three Yale buildings sat lay empty and dismal, a small cemetery plot encasing its live inhabitants. But nothing could keep out the outside world, an ever-growing turmoil.

Each passing week brought news of another British offense, another tax on the colonies, the taking away of trial by jury, another newspaper closed for objecting to Parliamentary legislation.

Two Yale tutors, John Trumbull and Timothy Dwight, kindled the sparks of patriotism among the students, challenged them to lift their voices and guns for liberty if need arose. Dr. Daggett's speeches in morning chapel turned sparks into flame, as he demanded the assembled young men "stand ready to meet your God with a pure heart and brave spirit, if you are forced into battle."

Talk of increased numbers of British redcoats filtering into the colonies replaced discussions of Cicero's essays and Greek logic. "It's all a matter of time," tutor Trumbull mumbled often, during the early months of 1775. "War steps closer with each passing day."

On the morning of April 21, 1775, Dr. Daggett's voice thundered in the chapel. He brought news of two days before when eight-hundred British troops had headed across the countryside to Concord, New Hampshire, to confiscate bullets and cannon stored by the colonists. Musket-carrying farmers had attempted to block their path at Lexington, only to fall victims to British gunfire. Noah Webster leaned forward, listening to every word. With or without details, one point was clear—war had come.

College students were exempt from military service, but that did not lessen their interest and enthusiasm about the Revolutionary War effort. Each day brought another bulletin of colonial militia groups forming, and efforts of British soldiers to put down group meetings and silence outspoken leaders. During his visits home, Noah shared moment-by-moment descriptions of Dr. Daggett's morning presentations. Mrs. Webster was disturbed by this.

"I think it sacrilegious to use the chapel for such discussions," she said with unusual firmness. "I had understood the good Dr. Daggett is a Doctor of Divinity. Perhaps he should be reminded that a chapel is a house of prayer."

"Oh, we do pray," Noah insisted. "We pray that God will help us in our--"

Noah stopped mid-sentence, realizing that he had already said too much. One glance at his father confirmed the matter, and a return look at his mother caught her with a clear and uncommon glare.

"I hardly think it prayerful to ask God to take sides in such matters," Mrs. Webster declared. "We each have enough to do in our personal wars against Satan. There is where we might find God on our side."

Master Webster coughed slightly as he always did before saying something important, "Ah, my kind Mercy, but let us not forget Exodus 15:3.'*The Lord is a man of war*'." Noah smiled broadly, grateful for his father's support—and memory.

"And then there is I John 4:8,"answered Mrs. Webster, "which says *God is love.*" And we might ponder Psalm 68:30 '*Scatter thou the people that delight in war.*' Surely we have not forgotten Isaiah 32:17.'*The work of rightousness shall be peace.*' Shall I continue?"

Master Webster shook his head. As well as he knew his Bible, he knew that his wife could claim even greater knowledge and understanding.

As for Noah, Jr., he gazed at both his father and mother with fresh love and respect. It was too bad that the colonies and England could not disagree like his parents, always mending their arguments upon conclusion. But sadly enough, it was not the case.

5

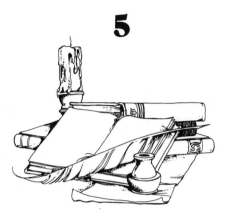

Choosing A Path

Touched by patriotic fever, the students at Yale
organized their own military company and drilled with
the New Haven militia. Noah brought the family flute
from home, quickly mastered a few favorite spirited
marches, and paced the drillers on the green.

On June 28, 1775, news of two important visitors
traveled across the Yale campus. "It's General George
Washington and General Charles Lee on their way
to take over the American Army at Cambridge," Dr.
Daggett announced at morning chapel services.
"They'll be staying the night at the home of Mr. Isaac
Beers and leaving in the morning."

All day long the Yale campus buzzed with the news.
It hardly seemed right that the dignitaries would leave
without some appropriate send-off. Early in the
morning of June 29, when the two noted generals left
the Beers' home and prepared to mount their horses,
their eyes widened in surprise. Before the house stood
uniformed soldiers and militiamen, ready to provide
an impressive escort out of the city. Noah opened the

march with a rousing playing of "Yankee Doodle" and the drummers joined him. It was a grand parade, which left Washington and Lee smiling and waving to show their appreciation.

Geography was added to Noah's program during his second year at Yale, joining Latin, Greek, Divinity, rhetoric and geometry. Master Webster could not hide his concern over his son's lack of interest in agriculture. It became more and more obvious the elder Webster had hoped Noah would find new and better ways of farming. After all, he had taken a second mortgage on the homestead for that purpose. But the thought did not appeal to young Noah. His mind found joy in the worlds of philosophy, politics, literature and science. Someone else could plow the soil, graze the livestock and feed the chickens. He did not show interest in business either, a second choice if Master Webster were choosing.

"If you do not wish to farm, perhaps you might clerk in a store and someday own it yourself," the father told his son. "There is always need for good merchants."

Noah, Jr., shook his head. "I'll not be answering that need, I'm afraid. Ordering stock and counting figures would give me little happiness."

"But what will you do with your education? You seem to learn without direction or purpose. One must pick a vocation."

"In time," the son said, with more than a trace of arrogance in his voice. "I'm afraid you could not understand, never being a college student yourself."

It was such an attitude that Noah came to use all too often. It hurt his father, pushing a distance between the two men. It would only grow wider as time went along.

Wider, too, grew the division between the colonies and England. In July of 1776, the Declaration of Independence brought the Yale students to their feet cheering as they gathered in chapel. Day after day, students carried the moving phrases on their lips: "When in the course of human events"…"We hold these truths to be self-evident"…"Life, Liberty and the Pursuit of happiness…" They were a call to arms, an explosive challenge to free men to stand up and be counted, a litany of abuses imposed by Mother England, a testimony in courage and noble intent. Yale students were swallowed up in the context of the powerful Declaration, yet to Noah Webster, Jr., it was even more. Never had he read a document of such eloquence and purpose. From the weekly news journal, he copied the document word for word, marveling at the magnificent phrasing, every word living and breathing freedom on the page. And on July 24, 1776, he sat transfixed as Timothy Dwight delivered the Valedictory Address to the graduating seniors.

"You should by no means consider yourselves as members of a small neighborhood, town or colony only, but as being concerned in laying the foundation of American greatness. Your wishes, your designs, your labors, are not to be confined by the narrow bounds of the present age, but are to comprehend succeeding generations, and be pointed to immortality."

Noah looked around, watching the intent faces as they listened to Dwight's speech. Did they grasp the meaning of what he was saying, these farmers and shopkeepers? The speaker continued, "You are to act, not like inhabitants of a village, nor like beings of an hour, but like citizens of a world, and like candidates for a name that shall survive the conflagration. These views will enlarge your minds, expand the grasp of your benevolences, ennoble all your conduct, and crown you with wreaths which cannot fade....Remember that you are to act for the empire of America, and for a long succession of ages.''

Again, Noah was caught up not only in the content of what was said, but in the beauty of words themselves, of language able to swell emotions, stir creative thought, offer direction and confidence.

The next month, when typhoid fever closed the school, Noah hurried home to West Hartford to join his father who was head of the local militia. He joined the soldiers, experiencing not the glamour of war, but its ugliness. They fought no redcoats, but instead, their own aching bodies, as they drilled and marched. They slept along mosquito-infested lakes where tents had to be filled with smoke to fight off the insects in order for men to get to sleep.

Returning to Yale in November, Noah found four students housed where two had been earlier. Food was scarce too, and students were sent home due to lack of provisions. Such interruptions posed major obstacles to learning, and Noah found Yale more and more disappointing. He fell victim to smallpox which left him weakened but unscarred.

Lacking necessary food provisions as well as fearing British attack on the New Haven location, Yale administrators broke the school into separate units to continue study, in late April of 1777. The seniors headed to Wethersfield under Tutor Dwight's direction, the juniors, under Tutor Joseph Buckminster, and the sophomores under Professor Strong, attended classes in Glastonbury, while the freshmen, under Abraham Baldwin reported to Farmington. Buckminster was a dull, uninspiring leader, causing Webster and others to request Dwight as the class's tutor for their senior year. Attached to a petition was

Webster's own personal poetic tribute to the gifted
Dwight:

> *Those views extensive, that exalted mind*
> *That manly firmness, and that zeal refin'd;*
> *That sacred fire, which, like the electric blaze,*
> *Darts thro' each state and beams enlivening rays,*
> *Glow in your breast; you reach a fostering hand*
> *To nourish science and adorn*
> *the land.*

But Webster's attention turned from the Yale
campus to West Hartford in the summer of 1777. His
father was still in charge of the local militia, largely
composed of older soldiers, but also including Noah's
brothers, Abraham and Charles. News spread across
the countryside that General Burgoyne planned a
major attack on the colonial forces. Young Noah,
steeped in patriotic rhetoric, was glad to join his family
and friends in an effort to obstruct the Burgoyne
challenge. No flute did he carry this time, but a musket
ready to be fired. However, before he got the chance,
Burgoyne was forced to surrender, an event Webster
accepted as the turning point in the Revolutionary
conflict.

In November Noah Webster, Jr., returned to begin
his final year at Yale. Only the seniors occupied the
New Haven campus under the charge of a new
president, Dr. Ezra Stiles. The fifty-year-old Stiles was
as enthusiastic about learning as he was learned
himself. New life came to Yale, new feeling and thirst
for knowledge. Webster applied all his energy to his
studies, deciding that law would be his future vocation.
He was selected to present the Cliosohic Oration in
English at Commencement, held September 9, 1778.
It was an honor reserved for seniors in the top
scholastic quarter of their class who had distinguished

themselves in writing and speaking.

But if twenty-year-old Noah Webster, Jr., felt important at his Yale graduation, he was quickly brought back to reality at home. His father, having skimped and budgeted to give one son four years at college, could not understand why Noah, Jr. had no useable skill for earning a living. The study of law would demand more schooling, hence more money. There were those who studied law by actually working side-by-side with an attorney, but that too would require money for living expenses. Already in debt for his son's expenses at Yale, Noah Webster, Sr. decided enough was enough. It was not fair to Abraham and Charles to constantly support their brother.

"Take this," Master Webster told Noah, Jr., handing his son eight dollars in continental currency. The money was actually worth but two dollars. "You must

now seek your own living. I can do no more for you.''

A surprised and uncertain Noah, Jr. took the money and retreated into his room. For three days he hibernated, feeling complete discouragement. He read the words of Samuel Johnson and thought about his future.

''To fear no eye, to suspect no tongue, is the great prerogative of innocence, an exemption granted only to invariable virtue.'' So wrote the famous Dr. Johnson in *The Rambler*. Yes, Noah thought, it *is* good to be trusting of others, to offer them respect and kindness. By helping people, you, too, will be helped.

Finally, there was the tried and true maxim—''The Lord helps those who help themselves.'' Whatever Noah decided to do, he knew he would need to do on his own. His father had sacrificed enough.

''Lord, give me direction,'' young Noah Webster prayed in the quiet of his room. ''Allow me to choose a path in this world that will bring joy to you, honor to my family and purpose to myself.''

In three days a door opened. It was more than just the door to Noah Webster, Jr.'s bedroom. It was a door to the future, Emerging was a twenty-year-old graduate of Yale, still a bit unsure of himself, but ready to write a new chapter in his life.

6

"Come To Attention, Class!"

For the third time Noah rearranged the two books, the ruler, the quill pen and the ink bottle that sat on his desk. Sweat glistened on his forehead, He rubbed his palms into his pantaloons, trying hard to appear relaxed. But the effort was in vain. In moments the room would be filled with youngsters, each one looking to him for instruction.

The three days spent in hibernation the previous spring led Noah to make three big decisions. First of all, he knew it was time to make his own money and pay his own bills. Secondly, since there were school teaching positions available, Noah decided to find one. Finally, once he had saved enough money, he would try to become a lawyer.

"I would have thought you would have had enough of the classroom," Master Webster had said. "And to become a lawyer? Surely there is more honor in farming or shopkeeping . . ." Wanting no arguments, Noah had not replied.

He found himself a teaching spot in Glastonbury, where his Yale class had spent their junior year. He settled comfortably into a boarding house in the village, and readied himself for the first day of school.

Now that day was here. Noah walked to the front door of the one-room school house, took the handbell from a side table, stepped outside and rang it. He glanced at the church next door, whispered a soft "Be with me, Lord," and awaited the boys and girls who were starting a new term.

Within minutes, the room was filled with some fifty youngsters, ranging in age from six to sixteen. The younger students sat toward the front, the older "veterans" in the rear.

"Welcome to Glastonbury School," Noah began, his voice cracking a bit. "My name is Master Webster, and I shall be your teacher. I welcome that duty and I consider it an honor . . ."

The more Noah spoke, the stronger his voice

became. His fears slipped away as he became caught up in the tasks to be done. By the end of the first day, he noted proudly that he knew the names of half of the pupils in the room. Tomorrow he would learn the rest. Not only that, he had listened to every reading group.

Soon one day passed swiftly into the next, with the classroom constantly abuzz with activity. Clearly the students liked their young schoolmaster. Why, he could speak Latin as fast as they could speak English—and forcefully too! He read to them from the *Connecticut Courant*, keeping each mind aware of the latest Revolutionary War fighting. And he never ran out of fun word games, testing their vocabulary and teasing their humors.

"How many names begin with the letter *A*? When you've written those down, write the names that end with the letter *A*."

"My name does!" exclaimed Alexander. "I mean it begins with *A*!"

"Then begin with yourself," Noah answered.

"But shouldn't such a list begin with the name Adam?" a younger girl asked. "He was the first of us all."

Noah nodded. "Then begin your list with Adam. But Alexander may start with Alexander, if he wishes."

While it was evident the pupils at the Glastonbury village school liked their new teacher and that he liked them, too, Noah's desire to become a lawyer remained strong, What money he had after paying for room and board went for law books. However, the six-dollars-a-month salary was really inadequate to meet his needs.

As autumn slipped into winter, cold winds whistled between the logged walls at the schoolhouse. Boys and girls shivered as they passed the single copy of the Last Testament around for reading lessons. There was also only one speller for all fifty students.

When another teaching job became available in Hartford during the spring of 1779, Noah took it. Sadly enough, the conditions were about the same. Putting pen to paper, the schoolmaster wrote essays about the problems. He could not understand how people in the country could place such importance on education yet fail to support it with proper books and buildings. Noah spent more and more time studying law, using the library of Oliver Ellsworth, a prominent local attorney.

During the summer of 1780, Noah moved to Litchfield, Connecticut. He'd had enough of dingy, freezing classrooms. The County Recorder of Deeds, Jedidiah Strong, suffered from a variety of ailments and needed help with his office. It was just the opportunity Noah wanted. He could help the Recorder during the day and study law books at night.

Noah was not the only law student in town. Litchfield attracted men from across the northeast, many choosing to study with Tapping Reeve, a well-known law instructor. Noah had no funds for such an education. Instead, he learned on his own, sharing thoughts and ideas around the stove in Recorder Strong's office. Many of the arguments were hotter than the coals in the stove, and Noah did not hesitate to join in the discussions. Education was one of his favorite topics.

"It's up to the government to establish good schools, to make sure every boy and girl gets a proper chance to learn," twenty-two-year-old Webster insisted. "Everybody seems to think education is so important, but we do little with our schools."

"It's up to the villages and towns to run their own

schools," another law student declared. "There are too many other matters that are more important in this country."

Noah shook his head. "I can't think of one. I think education is the core of our country's strength."

Long into the night the talk went on. Noah welcomed the exciting discussions, but he worried at how many law students kept arriving in town. Was there enough legal work to keep all the future attorneys busy?

The duties handling legal papers in the Recorder's office gave Noah fine hands-on experience. At night, hunched over law books or debating judicial cases, he gained valuable help with theory. He sometimes forgot to eat and sleep, he was so caught up in the study of law. When he returned to Hartford in April of 1781 to take the bar examinations, his mother was shocked.

"You've become a scarecrow!" Mrs. Webster exclaimed. "Become an attorney if you wish, but with God's tender mercy, please become a live one."

Never was the stew in the Webster's pots so thick or the cornbread so heavily buttered. Law tests or no law tests, no son of Mercy Steele Webster would be seen in public with bones protruding from his body. Within days, Noah's skin wore a rosier glow and he walked with a sure, poised swagger. He took the bar examinations with confidence, being little surprised when he learned he had passed them. It gave him the right to sign his name Noah Webster, Jr., Esquire. But sadly enough, it did not put money into the bank. Nor did it repay the six hundred dollar debt he still owed his father from college.

Again, it was time for making decisions. The Revolutionary War was all but over. Only the ceremony of British surrender remained. Yet there was little, if any demand for young attorneys who could claim no legal chambers or reputation. Farming? No, he wanted none of that. Clerking, too, was not attractive. In the midst of his thinking, Noah found a Bible verse returning to him often. It was from I Timothy 4:14 which stated, *"Neglect not the gift that is in thee."* Teaching. Of course, that was it. Deep inside, Noah knew he was called to instruct, to share learning. "But this time, it will be different," he promised himself. "I shall run my own school."

Sharon, Connecticut was the town he chose. Located in Litchfield County, the community boasted many wealthy families. Surely they would appreciate the talents of a valuable schoolmaster. To collect pupils, Webster placed an ad in the *Connecticut Courant*.

> *The subscriber, desirous of promoting Education, so essential to the interest of a free people, proposes immediately to open a school at Sharon, in which young Gentlemen and Ladies may be instructed in Reading, Writing, Mathematics, the English Language, and, if desired, the Latin and Greek Languages — in Geography, Vocal Music, etc., and at the moderate price of Six Dollars and two thirds per quarter per scholar. The strictest attention will be paid to the manners and the morals of youth, by the public's very humble servant,*
>
> NOAH WEBSTER, *Jun.*
>
> *P.S. If any persons are desirous of acquainting themselves with the French Language, they may be under the instruction of an accomplished master in Sharon.*

Thirteen pupils enrolled in Noah's class. Governor John Cotton Smith offered his spacious attic for the sessions which began July 1, 1781.

Sadly enough, the optimistic young schoolmaster soon discovered learning was not always a matter of having enough books and comfortable quarters. Attitude was important too. The students showed little respect for their instructor. He was clearly a common

man. It showed in his clothing and manner. He had
no wit, no cleverness. All he knew were facts and
figures. There was never a moment's merriment. The
only laughter in the attic was that aimed at the
schoolmaster.

One morning in October, Noah arrived at school
early. He was eager to share news of the British
surrender at Yorktown. Commander Cornwallis had
met General Washington and admitted defeat. The
Revolutionary War fighting was over.

"What's this?" Noah said, lifting a round shaped
object wrapped in light paper. Why, it felt like an
apple. One of the pupils must have brought it early.
Smiling, and glancing about the attic classroom for
a spying young face, Noah stripped off the paper. His
face winced. Yes, indeed, it was an apple. As green
as Connecticut grassland it was, except for the squishy
brown bruises. Ah, there was one large worm's hole.
Noah held the apple closer, examining the tiny inked
letters beside the opening. "Master Webster's Home"
the printing read.

Noah plopped down in his chair. He suddenly felt
very sick, and at the same time, he felt angry. Did
none of his pupils understand how hard he was
working to teach them? Was this the thanks he was
due?

On October 9, 1781, Noah packed up his suitcases
and closed the school in Sharon after only one quarter
of teaching. Again, he was tired of the classroom. At
twenty-three, he felt very old and tired. Thankfully,
however, he carried with him the awareness that he
was not alone. Once more, Noah sought direction.
"Be with me, Lord. Lead me to the path you would
have me follow."

7

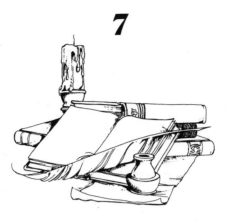

Where To Go?

"I'm sorry, Mister Webster. If you'd had some actual experience as an attorney on your own, we might be able to find something for you to do."

"Never clerked at all in any shop or store? We really don't have time to bring in new help now that the war is over."

Yes, the Revolutionary War fighting was finished, but for Noah Webster, Jr. another battle was being waged. Colonists struggled to rebuild villages destroyed during the years of bloody encounter. Once-rich farmland had gone to seed, deserted by those who set aside their plows for muskets. The cost of freedom had been high.

"Sorry, Mister Webster . . ." Again and again Noah heard the words repeated. He traveled from town to town, hoping that there might be one storekeeper willing to take him on, or perhaps a small law office which needed a clerk.

But slowly soldiers filtered back to their homes after the war. Family and friends reached out in gratitude,

finding jobs for the ex-fighting men to do. Now and
then Noah thought of returning to West Hartford.
Surely his family would take him in. Yet he would
be one more mouth to feed. No, Noah promised
himself that he would no longer be a burden to his
family. Only when he was ready to pay more of the
debt from college would he be able to face his father
again.

Even as he desperately looked for work as a business
or legal clerk, thoughts of what was wrong with
education in the country whirled in Noah's head. He
penned his thoughts in essays, now and then leaving
one in a newspaper office for publication. He spoke
out in other directions too, sharing his personal views
about the role of government in the new nation.
Clearly, the Articles of Confederation were no longer
effective in holding together the new and free colonies.
Talk was already in the works for a gathering of
leaders to spell out the goals and responsibilities of
the independent nation.

"It is essential that the new government provide
for a national system of education," Noah wrote,
"whereby each and every citizen may acquire the skills
of reading and writing. At the core of this system shall
be fundamental precepts of patriotism and morality,
which will strengthen the individual human spirit
while strengthening the nation itself."

The winter of 1781 was cruel and grim for Noah
Webster, Jr. By spring, he had returned to Sharon
once again. He paid another visit to the offices of the
Connecticut Courant, requesting that the following
advertisement be placed:

> *On the first of May will be in Sharon in Connecticut, a*
> *school, in which children may be instructed, not only in the*
> *common arts of reading, writing, and arithmetic, but in any*
> *branch of Academical literature. The little regard that is*

*paid to the literary improvement of females, even among
people of rank and fortune, and the general inattention
to the grammatical purity and elegance of our native
language, are faults in the education of youth that more
gentlemen and ladies have taken pains to censure than
to correct. Any young gentlemen and ladies, who wish
to acquaint themselves with the English language,
geography, vocal music, etc., may be waited upon at
particular hours for that purpose. The price of board
and tuition will be from six to nine shillings lawful
money per week, according to the age and studies of the
Scholar; no pains will be spared to render the school
useful.*

Noah Webster

It was an essay as much as an ad, clearly setting
up the curriculum of a secondary school. It also carried
the schoolmaster's feelings that while many people
criticized education, those same people did little to
solve the problem. There seemed little doubt that
Noah Webster planned to change the situation.

But sadly enough, Noah did not get the chance.
Since his departure the previous October, parents had
found other schools for their youngsters. Those who
had children who might have enrolled were told that
he had been "a good and thorough" teacher, but had
only stayed for a one quarter term. After the
disquieting wartimes, most people sought a sense of
security. Who could promise that this Webster fellow
might again pack his bags in a few months?

Disappointed but not ready to give up, Noah
headed south. The war had not been as hard on the
land and buildings there. A rattling stagecoach took
him to Newburgh were he was ferried across the river.
By the time he reached Goshen, New York, he could
go no further. Only seventy-five cents tinkled in his
pants pocket. His inquiries about work in the area
revealed there was only one possibility—teaching at
the Goshen high school.

"I hear tell the pay is ten dollars a month," offered one shopkeeper.

"In what form of currency?" Noah asked. Money that had been printed by the Continental Congress was of questionable value. So was the paper money produced by individual states during the Revolutionary War fighting.

"Silver coin," came the answer.

With that, Noah Webster investigated the matter more deeply. Within days, he was hired. It felt good to be back in a classroom again, enjoying the thrill of young people learning. At night, he turned his attention to his own writing. Already he had written essays about the problems of education in America— poorly equipped buildings, inappropriate furniture, not enough books and supplies. But anyone could be a critic. It was easy to find what was wrong with something. The tough part was trying to find solutions. Noah decided to start with dismantling the old Dilworth spelling and language book. It was no small target.

Since 1750, Thomas Dilworth had reigned supreme in the colonial classroom. His rules of orthography, pronunciation and usage were accepted without question. People of education and culture, wishing to make a point about proper language, used Dilworth as the ultimate authority. When the new Goshen schoolmaster shared his thoughts about writing another textbook, most people shook their heads in doubt.

"Who needs another speller?" a friend asked.

"We do!" Noah insisted. "We are a new nation. The Dilworth book recites praise for this British king and that British queen. We are Americans, free and independent. And why should our students learn the towns and rivers of England? Should our young people not know their own country?"

"But the Dilworth volume contains lessons of faith, of the dangers of the devil and wickedness—"

"So, too, shall mine, with a bit more flavor toward the joy of being noble and good and a bit less emphasis on the punishments of being evil."

Noah found little support. If the job would be done, he would have to do it himself. At night in his boardinghouse, he worked into the early morning hours, the wax of candles forming small mountains on his table. When his writing hand grew weary and his back ached from sitting, he was reminded of a thought from Ecclesiastes 9:10. "*Whatsoever thy hand findeth to do, do it with thy might.*" The words strengthened him; made him push onward.

Page by page the book grew. It began with lists of simple syllables and sounds, then moved ahead to basic words and phrases. There was a chart listing

cities and towns in the United States, and important
dates and events in American history were included.
When he felt he had enough to show, Noah took it
to the parents of his pupils. They were impressed!

"It's a remarkable effort," offered one father. "You
must be exhausted."

Noah was. In January of 1783, he recorded the toll
the book had taken on him. "I have sacrificed ease,
pleasure, and health in the execution of it, and have
nearly completed it. But such close application is too
much for my constitution. I must relinquish either the
school or writing grammars."

The school it would be. Binding his manuscript
together, he headed north. It was not enough to have
praise from the Goshen parents. He needed the
endorsement of notable educators and politicians.
From the former, he wanted approval of his
instructional techniques. From the latter, he wanted
assurance of a copyright. If he was going to do all this
work, Noah wanted to know his efforts were useful
and going to be protected.

Happily, the schoolmaster received the approval he
sought. Patriotic legislators like Thomas Jefferson and
James Madison recognized the importance of instilling
national pride in young people, while professors at
the University of Pennsylvania and Princeton hailed
Noah's use of one New England form of word
pronunciation as "general custom" usage.

Not that Webster did not encounter obstacles. At
twenty-four, he was automatically challenged by those
suspicious of youth. Who was *he* to put together a
textbook? Noah would not be intimidated.

"I saw a need and I believe I have answered it.
Must all wisdom come with age?" With some degree
of smugness, even arrogance, Noah rubbed his chin.
"Might I remind people of a certain young boy many

years younger than I who was found teaching his elders in the temple long ago? I would think not."

Those listening exchanged bewildered looks. Surely the young man before them would not compare himself to the Lord Jesus? Yet there were times when Noah seemed driven with the same force and determination.

"Master Webster, you have taught school," noted one observer during a presentation. "How will you discipline a child who does not learn his lessons—or perhaps, the lessons you have here provided?"

Noah shook his head. "I would prefer to *reward* the child who *does* learn. Too long we have held a rod or strap over those in the classroom. This does not make a child learn."

"But does the fear of the devil and Hell keep a child from sin?" asked another.

"I would think God would rather have us lift a child's spirit by offering him eternal life in Paradise through the goodness of the life he leads."

Not all those Noah met agreed with his thoughts, but most were impressed with his energy and courage. Carefully Webster wrote down suggestions people gave him for his text. Although the core was spelling, the final manuscript contained geography, history, manners, fables, science, and a "bit of everything" as Noah like to say. He called his work *"The American Instructor."*

"No, no, no," declared his former Yale president Ezra Stiles. "Too common, too ordinary."

Thus, Noah's offering became *A Grammatical Institute of the English Language.* Further, it claimed to comprise "An easy, concise & systematic Method of Education, designed for the Use of English Schools in America." Personally, Noah felt the title was a bit too pompous, yet who was he to argue with such a noted educator as President Stiles?

Noah struggled with the moral content of his manuscript. Many short directives were offered, both to build language skills and character.

> *Be a good child; mind your book; love your school, and strive to learn.*
> *Tell no tales; call no ill names; you must not lie, nor swear, nor cheat, nor steal.*

For those pupils who might not pick up the advice on their first reading, Noah repeated the lesson in a complete paragraph:

> *A good child will not lie, swear nor steal. He will be good at home, and ask to read his book; when he gets up, he will wash his hands and face clean; he will comb his hair, and make haste to school; he will not play by the way as bad boys do.*

Just as the readings grew a bit longer, a bit deeper, so, too, did the spelling lessons. Beginning with sound patterns—ba, be, bi, bo, bu, they soon took on actual word forms—bag, beg, big, bog, and bug. By the end of the book, pupils were learning to spell such proper words as Abraham, Beelzebub, Dionysius, Catawba, Appalachian and Ticonderoga.

Not only did Webster feel his book should outline good moral direction, he wanted a strong spiritual base to be its foundation. But he refrained from constantly referring to the name of God as other texts had done. "Nothing has greater tendency to lessen the reverence which mankind ought to have for the Supreme Being than a careless repetition of His name upon every trifling occasion," Webster insisted.

Although Noah discarded the Deity usage, he was determined to keep faith and religion as major ingredients of his manuscript. Carefully, with the simplest of words and most eloquent of meaning, he recorded the history of the creation of the world.

In six days God made the world, and all things that are in it. He made the sun to shine by day, and the moon to give light by night. He made all the beasts that walk on the earth, all the birds that fly in the air, and all the fish that swim in the sea. Each herb, and plant, and tree, is the work of His hands. All things, both great and small, that live, and move, and breathe in this wide world, to Him do owe their birth, to Him their life. And God saw that all the things He had made were good.

But as yet there was not a man to till the earth. Then God created Adam, the first man, and give him rule over all that He had made. And the man gave names to all the beasts of the field, the fowls of the air, and the fish of the sea. But there was not found a helpmeet for man; so God brought on him a deep sleep, and then took from his side a rib, of which he made a wife, and gave her to the man, and her name was Eve: And from these two came all the sons of man.

Writing the book was no easy task. But Noah had no idea how difficult it would be to get it published. That battle was only beginning.

8

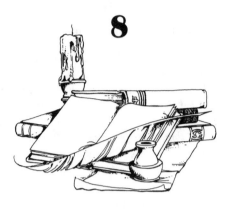

Touching Young Lives

By the time Noah completed his speller text in 1783, he was exhausted. Yet there was no time to rest. He was eager to get it into the classrooms of America. He soon discovered it was not an easy process.

No books had even been published in America. They had all come over from other countries. Therefore, there was no established pattern of getting a book published in the entire nation. Nor was there any protection for a book if it did find publication.

Caught up in the patriotic fervor of a newly-born country, Noah Webster, Jr., had no intention of seeking publication of his manuscript abroad, His speller was American to the core, bursting with a spirit of pride and excitement. The author was delighted with his effort and he would not turn it over to vultures or pirates who would copy it, print it, and not pay Noah for his hard work.

Carefully Noah charted a course of action. Assembling the letters of introduction and recommendation he had accumulated, he headed by horseback and

stagecoach to the major cities in the northeast. He met
with members of state legislatures, asking for copyright
laws to be passed so his work could be protected. He
also talked with school teachers, showing them his
manuscript and enlisting their support. All were
impressed with the twenty-five year-old Webster, his
writing and his enthusiasm. By Christmas,
Connecticut, Massachusetts, Maryland, New Jersey,
New Hampshire and Rhode Island had each passed
laws offering protection for American authors.

With renewed energy, Noah began seeking some
way to get his speller circulated. Although all those
who saw the work praised the manuscipt, none had
the money to cover the printing costs. After all, a war
had just been fought. People were only starting to
rebuild their lives and businesses.

"You may have to pay for the printing yourself,"
a friend told Noah.

There was little chance of that. What few funds
Noah had managed to save while teaching, he had
passed along to his father. If only someone, anyone,
would be willing to print but 5000 copies of the
manuscript, Noah was sure the money would be
quickly regained.

Thankfully, two Hartford men were willing to do
just that. Barzillai Hudson and George Goodwin,
publishers of the *Connecticut Courant*, invited Noah to
a business meeting in the newspaper offices.

"We think your manuscript has potential,"
Goodwin offered, rubbing a rather pointed nose, "and
we're willing to publish 5000 of the speller without
any investment from you."

Noah leaned forward, soaking up every word.

"If the book makes money, everything is fine,"
added Hudson, "If not, we'll expect you to pay the
total bill for our printing."

This time Noah leaned back, pondering the significance of what the two men were offering. He desperately wanted to see his manuscript in print. It was so much better than what was being used. But what if it did not sell? He would likely spend the rest of his life paying back the debt . . . and he still owed his father for college.

Goodwin and Hudson exchanged looks. This was a project they wanted to do. But being businessmen, they had no desire to throw time and money away.

"If you were a well-known educator," Goodwin offered, "It might be different."

"Or if your family was of some prominence." added Hudson.

The remarks did not sit well with young Noah Webster, Jr. His eyes sparked, "Or if I were a few decades older, or if I knew important people. Well, gentlemen, I have none of these things. I only have a manuscript I think worthy of publication. . . . and faith. But is it not the Book of James that reads, *Faith, if it hath not works, is dead?* I think it so. Therefore, put the presses to work. I believe we have a speller to print."

Handshakes and smiles were exchanged. The work began. In October of 1784, the first copies of a *A Grammatical Institute of the English Language* made their debut, Wrapped in a blue cloth coat, each volume of 119 pages, was priced at one shilling, two-pence.

From mercantile to hardware store Noah traveled, asking store owners to stock his book. It did not matter if they had never sold books before. The enthusiastic Webster simply displayed his smile and charm.

"I don't care where you put them—with the nails or cloth or medicine—just put them somewhere. I think you'll find people might take to the books."

And to the schoolmasters, he carried the text, with

a plea to try them with their pupils. "Having stood in a classroom myself, I think I know what you need," he told them. "I hope you'll give my text a try."

Many schoolmasters did just that, and the results came in quickly. Students liked the new word and name lists—"pure American" they were! Schoolmasters reported seeing changes in their students. Learning was almost—almost fun!

Before long, the Webster speller was making its way into the hands of parents as well—adults who had grown up using only the Dilsworth text. Webster's manual seemed brighter, more cheerful. Fathers and mothers eagerly shared their children's lessons, memorizing the spelling and meaning of new words, discussing the moral of the stories, building upon the spiritual reflections.

"You sure helped make our job easier," one preacher told Noah. "Your book backs up everything we try to tell the folks from the pulpit. We're obliged to you."

One store owner brought more good news. "I'm selling almost as many of your spellers as I'm selling Bibles," he told Noah.

The happy author smiled. "I shall never mind being second in sales to the Good Book."

In nine months, the first 5000 copies were sold. Quickly the second press run was ordered. Why not add some pictures, Noah thought, to decorate the pages? Children enjoy illustrations. Since the first book emphasized spelling, perhaps the next edition could provide more grammar. After all, too many Americans relied on what they heard to be correct. "Sounds right to me!" most people would say. But what *sounded* right to one person may sound wrong to another. Rules were needed—Laws of Language— aimed at helping develop standard speaking and writing in the country. Next should come a reader—a collection of fables and stories putting the spelling words and the language laws into use; a book that would both educate and entertain. Yes, Noah knew he had much work ahead of him. He set to the task at once.

But first Noah visited his father. The 5000 copies of the speller that were sold paid back Hudson and Goodwin, allowing Webster one hundred and thirty-six dollars of his own. From his meager teaching earnings, Noah had been able to share only a few shillings now and then with his family. Now he could pay dollars! The money was welcomed by Master Webster, Sr. He smiled, clearly proud of his son who had not forgotten his debt.

Despite his love for words, Noah did not want to submerge himself completely with his writing. He still wanted to practice law. Finding a comfortable boarding house in Hartford, he gave notice that he was available and eager for clients. But in truth, there were more than enough attorneys looking for work and Noah Webster, Jr., attracted little notice. He had plenty of time to pursue his writing.

Noah did just that. He directed his time and attention to the second volume of his *Grammatical Institute*. The first had offered proper spelling and punctuation of words. The second aimed at putting the words together. It was designed in a question-answer format:

What is Grammar? *Grammar is the correct manner of using words to write and to speak.*

What is a Sentence? *A sentence is a collection of words that convey a clear meaning of thought.*

Following the correctly stated questions and answers

were short exercises full of mistakes for the pupils to catch:

> Philadelphia are a large city, it stand on the west side of the river Delaware, and am the most regular city in America.

Once the individual grammar rules were learned and short sentences corrected, it was time to really put the language student to the test. Noah included mismatched and muddled stories for boys and girls to rethink and rewrite.

> *One upon a time a goose feed its young by a pond side; and a goose, in such circumstances, be always proud and punctilious. If any other animal, without the least design offend, happen pass that way, the goose be immediately at it. The pond, she says, be hers, and she maintain her right in it and support her honor, which she have a bill hiss, or a wing flutter. In this manner she drive away ducks, pigs and chickens; nay even the insidious cat be seen to scamper.*

Once Noah finished the manuscript that he hoped would develop basic grammar skills, it was time to develop a story book. What fun Noah had with that one! Eagerly he shared the stories of America that he wanted young boys and girls to enjoy. He wrote of Columbus and the discovery of America, of its hills, rivers and valleys, the story of the Revolutionary War and the Declaration of Independence. Truly, Noah Webster offered an inspiring look at his new nation.

"But what of other countries?" a person might ask. "Is America the only place to have a geography?"

"Was there never any good writing to come from England?" another might wonder. "There are no British writings in the entire reader."

Of course, there were other countries. Certainly England had fine writers who could have been included in the Webster reader. But Noah was filled with the patriotic spirit and love that directed all he did. His love was the United States of America, independence newly-won, and ready to write its own history. But it was not enough to merely fill schoolbooks. Noah shared his thoughts with newspapers too. Sometimes he used his own name, other times he created a fictional name.

"Now why would you do that?" his mother wanted to know.

Noah smiled. "I'm afraid folks will get a bit tired of reading what I have to say," he answered. "It seems I never run out of words."

That was certainly true. He never ran out of words—or ideas.

Convinced of the need for a strong national government to replace all the loosely-tied state governments, Noah put those thoughts on paper too. A strong national government could provide a quality army and navy, raise taxes to help the people, print money that had equal worth everywhere, operate a mail service. There was so much that could be done! Noah published his ideas in a pamphlet called *Sketches of American Policy*, then traveled by stagecoach taking copies to every town and city he could find. Not everyone agreed with Noah.

One night, as Noah sat riding, he heard shots ring out. Immediately the coach driver pulled his horses to a halt. Webster's head pounded. He fumbled inside his waistcoat for his money pouch. If the men stopping the coach were bandits, they might not be satisfied with the moneybox the driver was carrying.

"Do you have a passenger by the name of Noah Webster?" a voice called out.

Noah shuddered. What would the men want with him?

"Who wants to know?" the driver shot back.

"You'll do much better to answer our questions than to ask those of your own," the man said sternly.

Frightened, but not wanting the driver to suffer any harm, Noah leaned out of the coach door. "I am Noah Webster," he said, his voice trying to hide the fear he felt.

"So you're the one. What right do you have speading your worthless pamphlets all over? Trash is what they are—misguided thoughts of a crazed idiot!"

Noah could feel his heart thumping in his head. Cold sweat covered his body. But he would not listen to such an attack. "You are entitled to your ideas. I have my own. Now, if you are finished, we will—"

"No, I'm not finished. You would destroy every government of each state, and build another monarchy over us, just as we fought to get rid of."

"I would do nothing of the kind!" Noah replied. "I would have a strong national government that would help all the citizens of this nation. This government could bring the states together and help them with benefits and services for the people."

"That's not what I have been told."

Grabbing the box that rested on the seat beside him, Noah slipped several of the pamphlets out. "Do not believe what you hear. Believe what you read. Take these. Study them. Then, if what I have said is not true, find me again."

Leading his horse closer, the driver stooped to retrieve the pamphlets. "And how might we find you?"

"One week from tonight I shall be riding this stagecoach out of Baltimore on this same road, I do not lie. If my thoughts are not what I claim them to be, you can track me down then.''

Up into the air the horse lifted its two front legs,
whinnying. ''I shall do that, Mr. Webster. For your
sake, I hope you have been truthful.''

With that, the driver galloped off, his two
companions close behind. Noah settled back into his
seat, breathing more easily. ''Thank you, Lord,'' he
whispered. ''And may I also pray that I have seen
the last of this fellow.''

After a busy week in Baltimore calling on
schoolmasters with his books, and legislators with his
pamphlet, Noah left the city. Thankfully, the
mysterious night riders did not reappear. Once again,
the stagecoach passenger offered a quiet grateful
prayer.

9

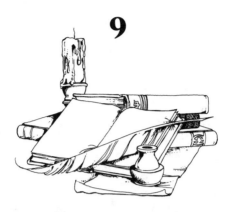

Meeting General Washington

An early morning May fog drifted lazily over the Virginia countryside. Now and then Noah halted the horse he rode, to give it a brief rest and to soak in the beauty of the surrounding fields and hills. In all of New England, never had there been such grand and beautiful scenery as this.

"He deserves it," Webster said aloud, standing in his stirrups and gazing in every direction. It was said that General George Washington owned some 70,000 acres of land in Virginia and another 40,000 in Maryland. Some 300 Negroes tilled the soil, tended the stables and serviced the Washington home at Mount Vernon. A glorious estate it was, yet no one in the nation held any malice for its owner. Lesser men would have chosen to lazily enjoy the leisure of a gentleman farmer's life, but more than once Washington had answered the call of his country and countrymen. Now that the battles were fought, he continued to serve. Talk circulated of a convention to be held, a meeting of colonial leaders to put together an official constitution for the new nation, Certainly, George Washington would play a major role.

It was such an awareness that brought Noah Webster on horseback to the Mount Vernon manor. In his vestcoat he carried letters of introduction, notes written by friends of the famed general in behalf of the schoolmaster author named Webster.

As Noah reached the front lane leading to the Mount Vernon house, his eyes widened. Never had he seen such a wide, sweeping home that sat majestically like a gem in the morning sun. As he drew his horse to a stop, a smiling Negro stableboy hurried out.

"I'll be taking your horse," the youth offered. "I'll see he's watered and dried down."

"Much obliged," answered Noah, dismounting and handling the boy the reins. "You wouldn't know if the General is at home?"

"No, sir, he rides this time each day. But he'll be coming home before long. Go on in. You'll be made comfortable."

That was an understatement, Noah discovered. Once inside the house, he was treated like visiting royalty. Servants darted here and there, each inquiring if there was anything he wanted or needed. Upon request, he was shown to the library where he stood in awe, gazing at the fine first edition volumes the master of the house had accumulated. He had just withdrawn a book about great Roman generals when the door to the side parlor opened.

Entering the room was a man of some 6'2'', 175 pounds with sandy-brown hair and blue eyes. His chin was pointed, his bearing straight and erect. "You, I am informed, are Master Noah Webster?"

Noah nodded. "And you are the honorable General George Washington."

Shaking his head, the man smiled. "The honorable is kind, but unnecessary. The General is in the past. I am merely George Washington, your servant and host."

The humbleness and graciousness of this master of Mount Vernon surprised Noah. Not that anyone had ever labeled the general "arrogant," but the thought of him being anyone's servant seemed ridiculous! Before Noah could say another word, he found himself invited for both lunch and dinner, with a further invitation to join the guests Washington had invited for the evening. Who would refuse? Certainly not an ambitious book promoter from New England!

With platters of fried chicken, mounds of whipped potatoes, goblets of fine wine, Noah enjoyed a king's feast. House servants stood attentive at every direction, eager to replenish portions, provide an extra linen napkin, or fulfill any wish. The ever-gracious Washington made each of his dinner guests feel duly important and comfortable, and what he might have momentarily neglected, his wife Martha supplied. How happy Noah was that he had remembered to pack a clean white shirt. It did not carry the fancied ruffles of others around the table, but it was acceptable. After dinner, the host and hostess of Mount Vernon led the way to the main parlor for songs and conversation around the piano. A more aggressive gentleman might have caught the wistful glances of the silked and satined young ladies in the party, but Noah was too caught up in the overall rapture of the evening.

It was late before Webster had an opportunity to display his school materials before General Washington in the library. Carefully he examined each one, holding pages near the blazing candles. Now and then he nodded, turning the page. Noah attempted to control his nervousness yet his palms were sweaty and he rubbed them into his pantalooned thighs.

"Your work has much merit," Washington finally offered. "Certainly a worthy accomplishment for a man of your years. You must be no more than—"

"I am twenty-seven, sir," Noah injected.

Washington rubbed his chin. "Well, you certainly have not wasted those twenty-seven years. You provide a fine approach toward language. We have much here in Virginia of which we are proud, but I'm afraid schools are not one of them. So often in New England your schoolhouses stand in the shadows of your churches, built at the same time. Good planning, I would say. Wise, indeed."

Was this the time to ask him, Noah wondered. Why not?

"Sir, your recommendation of my work would carry much public attention. If you look on my writing with favor, perhaps you would endorse my efforts . . ."

There, for good or bad, it was done. Noah scrutinized the man before him. It was impossible to interpret the General's reaction. Washington gazed into the fireplace, lost in the brilliant golds and oranges of the crackling logs. Finally, he faced Noah.

"Your words are kind, Master Webster, both those you speak here to me and these on paper. But I must refuse your offer."

"Yet you like what I have done—"

"Yes, indeed, although I am no educator, no schoolmaster. But a moment ago, I mentioned schoolhouses and churches. From your writing, I sense you are a man of God?"

Noah nodded. "I would like to think so."

"And I, the same," the General agreed. "Yet I

would not presume to endorse how you would pray to your God. Nor, I would imagine, would you assume to direct my own prayers . . .''

"Of course not.''

"Well, I respect what you have done here. These lessons would appear to be proper and useful means by which people could learn. But you are here to seek my name for your personal use with your work. A man's name is his honor, and I would not think it honorable to endorse work in which I have little professional knowledge. Nor would I tell you how to pray or worship simply because you believe in the Word of God as do I.''

As Noah lay in bed that night, he thought a long time about what General Washington had said. Perhaps, just perhaps, one could be over-zealous in his efforts, too eager to gain attention and acceptance. A verse from Ecclesiastes haunted his memory: "*The patient in spirit is better than the proud in spirit.*" Yes, there was much truth to that. Early the next morning, he bid his host a grateful farewell.

"I am only sorry I could not give you what you hoped I would,'' Washington said.

"You have given me a great deal more,'' Noah answered. "Perhaps I might leave this pamphlet with you. It's a few ideas I have about our new nation and its government.''

"That topic is always of interest to me. Um-m-m *Sketches of American Policy*. Sounds interesting. I shall peruse it today.''

"At your leisure,'' Webster replied.

The lesson provided by Washington settled in well for Noah. He remained as determined as ever to promote his language texts and his pamphlets about government. But rather than solicit personal endorsements constantly, he put together a lecture program. It contained a history of the English language, pronunciation rules, rules commonly broken, poetry, and the importance of education in America.

The first lecture on October 19, 1785, drew a crowd of only thirty listeners. Charging but three shillings a presentation, Noah worried. Naturally, he had to appear properly attired before a formal audience and this required adding to his wardrobe. Always conscious of his appearance, Webster rather enjoyed visiting a tailor or shoemaker. But he disliked renting a church hall or public meeting house when he had no idea what size the crowd would be.

Gradually, the audiences grew. Noah lectured with such intensity, such power, that those listening were swept up in the excitement of the moment. Many promised themselves to watch each word spoken, in private or public. Others debated the value of education established by a federal or state government. Seldom did the speaker crack a smile or share a humorous touch. Clearly he meant business, serious business. There were some who felt this young wizard of words took himself a bit too seriously. "Little monarch" he was called. "I do believe he would label it a sin if someone mispronounced a word," people said.

But people came to hear him speak, out of curiosity and interest. From town to town Noah took his talks, sharing his feeling about the government as well as language. From Maryland he headed to Virginia, then on to Pennsylvania. He managed to set up a meeting with Benjamin Franklin, another word wizard, who had championed the cause of liberty during the fight for independence. Not only did the eighty-year-old freedom fighter welcome a discussion about language, he was equally interested in Noah's thoughts about the federal government. The *Sketches of American Policy* pamphlet was well received.

"I am delighted you see the need for a central government which can pull the states together," observed Franklin.

"It's the only way our nation can survive," Webster answered. "If we would have but separate states without one unifying force, we would be no better off than all the individual countries in Europe."

"Indeed. But there are those who would challenge many points of your thinking . . . and writing."

Noah's jaw tightened. "I am ready to defend each of my thoughts, to the death, if need be."

His eyes twinkling over his low-resting spectacles, Franklin nodded. "Let us hope it need NOT be. But nonetheless, be prepared to support your thinking."

Webster found a receptive audience for his lectures in Philadelphia. Each presentation, six in all, attracted over one hundred people. Questions were many, discussion was lively. He hated to leave the city but he had scheduled presentations in Albany, Hartford, New Haven, Boston and other New England cities. He was happy to visit his family where he brought a handsome collection of gifts.

Once his lecture circuit was over, Noah sought work among booksellers and printers in New York City. It was a half-hearted effort at best. In his heart he had little interest in selling or printing books. He wanted to write them!

Shortly after Christmas in 1786, Noah found himself back in Philadelphia. The city was buzzing with talk about the forthcoming May meetings of colonial leaders. All thirteen colonies would be sending representatives to write a Constitution. "*The Articles of Confederation*" was too flimsy, too weak, to hold the states together in one union.

Noah knew Benjamin Franklin would have a major role at such a gathering. Like a doting son, Webster showered the elder statesman with constant attention. Together they spent hours simplifying language rules, They agreed silent letters sound be omitted in many words: bread to bred, give to giv, realm to relm. Letters with definite sounds replaced those that were vague: mean to meen, grieve to greev, speak to speek. Finally, short marks above letters could be added to differentiate sounds. (Most of these reforms fell by the wayside in actual practice, but the sharing sessions solidified the friendship—or "frendship"—between the two men.)

Noah hoped to be an active part of the proceedings taking place in Philadelphia for the writing of a Constitution. It was no small disappointment for him to find that the members of the Constitutional Convention were sworn to secrecy. But it was no secret that his own *Sketches of American Policy* pamphlet was in the hands of many of the delegates. From the time the convention began meeting in May of 1787 and through the summer, Webster dined with many of the representatives. In his diary he recorded visits with Franklin, Washington, James Madison, William Livingston, Roger Sherman, William Samuel Johnson, Oliver Ellsworth, Rufus King, Abraham Baldwin and Edmund Randolph. Often he found his thoughts the center of discussion. As the delegates wrapped up their duties in September, Noah received an unusual request. It came from a Pennsylvania representative, Thomas Fitzsimmons, who asked that Webster write an essay in support of the new Constitution.

"But I have not seen the document," said Noah.

"Trust me," answered Fitzsimmons. "You will approve of the final document."

Webster smiled, It was clear that many of his ideas had been included. "I shall be happy to oblige you, sir," he replied.

There was little doubt that Noah Webster carried quite a favorable opinion of himself. Not all shared such feelings. There were some who thought little of his notions that he could provide a better set of textbooks than Thomas Dilworth. Others took exception to his obvious overtures to befriend such leaders as Franklin and Washington. After all, who was he to write a pamphlet of American Policy? It was a sensitive and sad Noah Webster who wrote in his diary, "I have exposed myself to malice, envy, criticism, etc. by my publications. I knew I should when I began, and I am prepared for an attack on all sides."

Noah revealed much of his character within the pages of his diary. Entries show him to be energetic, ambitious, maybe a bit conceited, but always persevering and willing to share ideas—especially his own.

While Philadelphia was busy welcoming delegates to the Continental Congress in the spring of 1787, Noah Webster was busy with matters of his own. For the first time in many years, he set aside his concerns with reading, writing, and education. His interest in political matters waned a bit as well. The reason? A short, graceful belle from Boston, who brought a new, special joy into the life of Noah Webster, Jr.

10

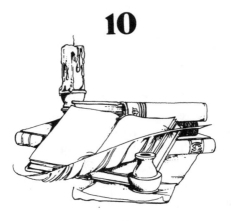

Bright Light From Boston

Her name was Rebecca Greenleaf, the daughter of William and Mary Greenleaf. Before the Revolutionary War, the name of William Greenleaf was well known among the merchants and traders of Boston. But the fight for independence, with its British blockade of the Boston port, had drained the family coffers. There was little left for William and Mary Greenleaf to share with their fifteen children, but their love and pride. From all accounts, that proved quite enough. As the Greenleaf sons and daughters left home to make their own way in the world, they commanded immediate admiration and respect.

Anne Greenleaf, sister of Rebecca, was no exception, and her marriage to Duncan Ingraham of Philadelphia was viewed by all as a ''heavenly union of two pure spirits.'' The Ingrahams entertained often, welcoming family and friends to their imposing red brick home in Pennsylvania's leading city. Happy in her own marriage, Anne was always willing to feed the fires of romance for anyone else. Sparks were struck when Noah first met Rebecca Greenleaf, who was visting her sister. Little outside help was required.

The progress of Noah and Rebecca's relationship was charted in Webster's diary. He noted on March 1 that he had been introduced to her. By the 7th of the month, she was "the sweet Miss Greenleaf." Two days later, she was "the agreeable Miss Greenleaf." By March 22nd, she was "lovely Becca."

Rebecca's brother James also became a trusted friend. Certainly, the shrewd Master Webster saw the value in having another ally in the Greenleaf family. Noah could hardly restrain his feelings for his new love, writing to James: "If ever there was a woman, moulded by the hand of nature to bless her friends in all connections, it is your sister Becca." Continuing his letter, the love-smitten Webster wrote, "To be united to her is not mere pleasure, bliss, felicity, it is more, it is a union that blends pleasure with delight with social advantages, it is a blessing. The man who loves her, loves the temper of saints, and by associating with her, must become a better man, a better citizen, a warmer friend. His heart must be softened by her virtues, his benevolent & tender affections must be multiplied. In short, he must be good, for he would be, in some measure, like her."

Becca was clearly as taken with Noah as he was with her. By the time she journeyed back to Boston in June, she carried a marriage proposal which she prayed her parents would bless. Having accepted a position teaching at the local Episcopal Academy, Noah encouraged his new love to take word home that he was ready to embark on greater, more important ventures.

"But there is nothing wrong with being a schoolmaster," Becca insisted.

Noah shook his head. "Please do as I request."

His spirit sailing with love for his beloved Becca, Noah hardly dreamed he could find greater happiness. But he experienced even greater joy when the new United States Constitution was revealed to the public. Within it, he saw many of his thoughts and ideas. He was delighted.

Yet the young patriot knew that not all Americans shared his delight. Many still felt the ultimate powers of government should rest at the state level.

"Without a strong union, a central federal government, the individual states would forever squabble among themselves for importance and power," Noah argued. "Certainly, there can be powers left to the state, but the federal government must hold the key of strength."

Always sure that he could express himself better on paper, Noah again took pen in hand. Pages of his feelings and thoughts poured out. He labeled his latest pamphlet *AN EXAMINATION INTO THE LEADING PRINCIPLES OF THE FEDERAL CONSTITUTION PROPOSED BY THE LATE CONVENTION HELD AT PHILADELPHIA.* He dedicated his work to his friend, Benjamin Franklin, and signed it "A Citizen of America."

Giving up his teaching duties, Noah devoted himself to getting the pamphlet printed and circulated. For the Constitution to become law, nine states had to ratify it. Webster pledged to do all he could to get the important document passed. He sent his pamphlet to all parts of the proposed union, talked to anyone who would listen and some who preferred not to, and wrote letters of support.

"If our mission fails," observed Franklin, "no one can blame Noah Webster. He has had as much to do with our efforts as anyone."

Eager to make Rebecca his bride, as well as make her family impressed with him, Noah started a new magazine in New York City. To raise money, he sold the rights to his speller and reader in New York, New Jersey and three other states. It was a poor business deal, with Webster receiving only two hundred dollars. But he was eager to begin.

THE AMERICAN MAGAZINE was a hodge-podge of articles and stories related to government, education, farming and philosophy. Soundly-written, with more than a mite of common sense, the features satisfied their readers. Sadly enough, however, there were too few readers. Noah poured what royalties he received from his other publications into his magazine, but it proved hopeless. In October of 1788 he gave it up.

"Thirty years of my life gone!" he recorded in his diary on his birthday. "I have read much, written much, tried to do much good, but with little advantage to myself. I will now leave writing."

Exiting the writing arena, Noah collected his best lectures and printed them. The handsome volume, called *DISSERTATIONS ON THE ENGLISH LANGUAGE*, met a response similar to his magazine. Those who read it, enjoyed it. Dr. Stiles, his longtime friend at Yale, was glowing. "We glory in a son of this Alma Mater that can be the author of such a learned production." There were a few criticisms, especially about the book's introduction, that Webster used a simplified spelling method to present. It made him think twice about trying to reform procedures that had been deeply entrenched within people's minds. But the final and disappointing result of the project was that Noah lost money on the venture.

Despite the failure of his publication, the lovestruck Webster could no longer stay away from Becca. He headed for Boston, where he restated his wish to marry her.

"I hesitate to ask your hand in marriage with such an unsure financial situation," Noah admitted, as the two sat on a couch in the Greenleaf home. "But my love for you is certain. It would be an adventure, that is true, if you are willing."

Becca smiled. "One does not love a moneybelt, whether it be thick or thin. Indeed, I am willing enough."

But brother James, who had taken Noah's side with the family, was not so eager. He had seen his father struggle through the war, watched the troubles that could come from lack of money. He urged caution.

"Love conquers many problems," James told Noah, "yet it does not feed an empty stomach. For the moment, my sister's thoughts are filled with you, whether you be rich or penniless, but I know her mind. She also enjoys that which a handsome purse provides. Be patient. Improve your fortune a bit."

They were not the words Noah hoped to hear, but he knew they were wise words indeed, "*I believe that patience is the most difficult virtue to acquire,*" he noted in his journal. "*For this servant of God, at least.*"

Unknown in Boston, Noah returned to Hartford. He was known in his own neighborhood, both as a lawyer and an author. If there be clients to seek him out, it would be in Hartford. He visited family and friends, making them aware he was "open for business" no matter how small a legal matter might need handling. For the first time, he carefully added up the amounts coming in from the royalties on his publications. By June of 1789, he wrote to James.

I think it best to marry as soon as a house can be obtained and furnished. For this we can depend wholly on your goodness; and the sooner you can make it convenient to assist your sister, the sooner you will make us happy. We have habits of economy and industry; but we are perhaps more ambitious to be good than great. It gives me some pain that Becca will have to leave her friends — friends which can nowhere be replaced. But no consideration can separate us, and she will cheerfully go where my interests lead me. For this, she is entitled to my warmest gratitude; indeed, I hardly know which she has the most of, my gratitude or my love.

Noah's love was clear, his intentions totally honorable. James Greenleaf wanted no part of standing in the way of his sister's happiness and his friend's dreams. He promptly turned over an order for one thousand dollars to provide the furnishings for a house. Noah had not expected so generous a dowry, and he was delighted to turn the money over to his wife-to-be. Becca had no trouble at all spending the amount, in fact, by the time she finished, not a shilling remained to furnish the kitchen.

"How easily the money flows through your fingers," Noah gently scolded. "I shall hope and pray we will not starve in our first year together."

"Oh, it will take me two years, at least," Becca answered, her dark eyes flashing. "The first year we will have plenty to eat."

On October 26, 1789, Rebecca Greenleaf and Noah Webster, Jr., were married in Boston. The Greenleaf home, the site for the wedding, resounded with laughter and happy chatter. The groom was 31, the bride 23. Noah noted in his diary, "*I am united to an amiable woman, and, if I am not happy, shall be much disappointed.*"

A month later, it was the groom's parents who entertained the new Mrs. Noah Webster, Jr. At times, she was not easy to find, for the tall, big-boned

Webster clan dwarfed the most recent addition to the family.

"It is a good-sized lot of people you have brought me to," Becca said.

Noah laughed. "For one who comes from a family of fifteen children, you would have to make your presence known."

Indeed, Becca did exactly that. Noah discovered with all her charm and beauty, his new bride enjoyed entertaining. Friends and relatives were invited often to the Webster house in Hartford, with the hostess spreading a grand table before them.

"I only wish the clients would beat a path to my law office as others we know enjoy the parties you offer," Noah told his wife.

"But at least you have plenty of time to write," Becca chimed back.

There was truth enough to that. Not only did Noah have time to write, to stay out of debt he had to. He published a series of short sermons in the *Connecticut Courant*, then put them into book form. They were tightly-structured little essays, each telling a story with a virtuous moral. Fearing some law clients might think his writing frivolous, he wrote under the name *The Prompter*.

"Humorous but with a message," one newspaper reader observed. "*The Prompter* accomplishes more in one column than any ten preachers do in ten Sunday homilies."

To share his political and patriotic views, Noah again used the *Courant*, this time calling himself *Patriot*. He spoke out strongly in behalf of state and city banks, emphasizing their economic strength within the new nation. In 1792, Hartford did organize a bank through the selling of stock but Noah himself could not afford to invest.

As Noah tried desperately to organize his finances from his extensive writing and meager law practice, Becca seemed equally determined to spend every penny. The birth of their first child Emily Scholten Webster, on August 4, 1790, was a mixed blessing. "She is truly a child of God," observed the baby's new father, "and we offer up thanks and praise." But with the prayer of thanksgiving, Noah was also hoping that his beloved Becca could find it within her to limit her spending. The arrival of yet another baby on February 5, 1793, reaffirmed the same wish. Frances Julia was a beautiful infant, healthy and with "a set of strong lungs." "*I am again in your debt, Lord,*" Noah wrote in his diary, "*as I seem to be with many others.*"

After four years in Hartford, the law office of Noah Webster, Jr., still struggled for survival. When an offer came to start a newspaper in New York City, Noah jumped at the chance. True, he had won election to the Hartford Common Council and the people of the town looked at him with respect for his writings. Yet respect did not pay bills. Therefore Noah packed up his family in November of 1793 and headed for New York City.

"It is an uncertain path I follow," wrote the new newspaper editor, "but as always, I shall put my life in the Lord's hands . . . and trust."

11

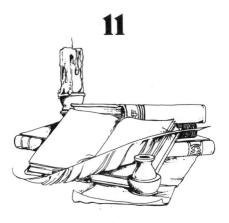

Under Attack

His forehead wrinkled with concern, Noah sat in a small office and listened to the men in the room, Alexander Hamilton, John Jay, Rufus King—each was a Federalist, sharing his thoughts about Webster's forthcoming newspaper. These men, and a few others, had put up loans of $150 to finance the venture.

On December 9, 1793, the first issue of *The American Minerva* appeared. As editor, Noah passed along many of the ideas of his investors. But even more importantly, he tried to back up his old friend, George Washington, who was struggling to put the United States on a solid footing.

"We cannot afford to concern ourselves with other countries," Webster wrote, "until we have achieved greater independence within ourselves. Let us remain neutral when other nations quarrel, and let us establish our own nation as an example for others to imitate."

Few Americans understood the unique power of the press more than Noah Webster, Jr. As his friends found their way to political power, he was always

willing to lend his support in writing when he agreed
with their ideas. He was equally willing to take the
opposing side, offering criticism when needed.
Thomas Jefferson was a frequent target of the Webster
pen:

> *There is little doubt that Thomas Jefferson loves his
> country, but he seems to love other countries with similar
> feeling. Should this gentlemen rise to greater position in govern-
> ment, let us hope that he remembers that he is an American
> first, and a gentleman of the world second.*

In 1797, Noah and Becca discovered a piece of the
country along the East River called Corlaer's Hook.
It was away from the busyness of the big city and
allowed Noah to have a garden. Though he had never
wished to be a farmer like his father, he enjoyed
planting seeds, pulling weeds, and watching the
magical way God brought life to the soil.

On April 6, 1797, God brought life to the Webster
home once again—another daughter, promptly
christened Harriet. "A man has little chance in a
home with four women," Noah moaned to his friends.
But his grey eyes twinkled in delight, he walked erect,
with pride in every step, and he maintained a tall,
slender figure and was handsomely dressed.

Each issue of the *American Minerva* carried the
distinct Webster imprint. He spoke out about
manners, education, politics—and, of course,
language. Ideas for city planning appeared, with
suggestions for how to keep the cities clean. He
proposed changes in laws, some newly-made and
others never considered. From forest conservation to
proper use of rivers and lakes, Noah spoke out.

"This Webster fellow seems to know about
everything," more than one reader commented.

Not all felt the editor's comments useful. Some
critics said his words had little real purpose. Other

critics took a more bitter tone. ''Quack!'' he was
labeled. ''A pompous peacock.''

The insults stung. But Noah would not answer his
critics in writing. ''People have a right to their own
opinions,'' he told Becca, ''no matter how foolish
those opinions might be.''

Not only did Webster comment and report events, he predicted them. When Prussia and Spain attacked France, Noah asserted the two countries would fail. They did. In 1797, he forecast that "some popular man who can attract around him a military superiority" would take over France. Enter Napoleon Bonaparte, who soon held the country in the palm of his hand.

"How do you know such things?" people asked.

Noah shook his head. "It is certainly no Divine power. The exact fulfillment of the prediction indicates nothing more than an ordinary share of historical knowledge, united with a candid comparison of all the circumstances and events."

The *American Minerva* was published every day but Sunday. Aimed at a general New York City readership, Webster introduced a sister paper, *The Herald*, which appeared semiweekly for a wider readership. The circulation of both newspapers continued to grow, topping 1700 by Noah's fortieth birthday in October of 1798.

But the newspaper work took its toll.

Late one night, as Noah made his way home, the sound of horse's hooves clattered behind him. He whirled around, only to confront a fuzzy night with no distinct shape. Instinctively, he stepped to one side as a horseman galloped by at great speed.

"Thank you, Lord," the dazed Webster whispered, feeling his body cover with a cold, clammy sweat. "Once more, I am in your debt."

A visit to his doctor revealed that Noah was working himself blind. Too little sleep, too much work. He seldom took time to eat and his thin body had little extra meat to sustain him.

With a wife and three children to support, Noah knew he had to get away from the schedule that was killing him. He gradually turned over the editor's duties to others. He retained ownership and the right to submit political columns.

But before he closed the door on newspaper life entirely, Noah made two promises. First of all, he resolved to become less personally involved with politics. He had little use for political parties, yet it was clear that the times had given birth to the Republicans and the Federalists. Webster was labeled a Federalist, and he did not like it. He drew away from Hamilton after he publicly criticized President John Adams. "There are too many greedy wolves in the political den," Webster wrote, "and they rip at the meat of the American nation." Secondly, Noah promised to do some writing about disease. Scarlet fever had almost killed his own children, epidemics popped up with too much frequency, and Noah pledged to turn his attention to this topic.

Whatever he planned to do, Webster was certain he did not want to remain in New York City. Everything was so hurry-scurry, hustle and bustle. The entire area was exploding with new buildings and added people. Once, just on a lark, he began counting houses on one city block. He counted sixteen hundred houses! Yes, it was all just too big.

A voice on the wind seemed to whisper, "Come home to Connecticut." It was a lure that Noah could not resist. But the struggles of life in Hartford remained in his memory. He did not want to go back to times when days would roll by with no sign of a law client.

But visiting in New Haven on business, Noah came upon a house. Facing the harbor, the white imposing structure seemed perfect for Becca's taste and sturdy enough to withstand three lively, growing girls. There was a garden in the back, with an orchard besides. A compact stable stood ready to accommodate a horse, feed, and a carriage.

"Why, it's a patch of Heaven on earth!" Becca exclaimed, upon seeing the New Haven house. "It would be a perfect place for you to write."

Noah nodded. "And should we decide to have more children, the house is adequate."

A light blush covered Becca's face as it always did when her husband mentioned having more children. But both of them knew their family was not complete as yet. Why, often Noah spoke of having ten—"the Good Lord be willing!"

Soon the wooden sign in front of the house read "Noah Webster, Jr., Esquire." Within weeks, they were so settled in, they felt like they had been there for years. Neighbors came calling, bringing fresh-baked pies and tarts. Many were surprised—and

delighted—when they learned their new friend had authored the speller and reader in their local school.

Once the social festivities calmed down, Noah returned to his writing. He had hoped to wash politics from his pen, but he could not ignore the feuding taking place between the outgoing President John Adams and the incoming President Thomas Jefferson. After all, a new century was beginning. Was this any way for a "united" nation, still in its crawling stages to behave? He attacked Jefferson for appointing supporters and friends to government positions. This spoils system was unfair, Noah asserted, and never should a man "receive position for *who* he knows rather than *what* he knows. Such thinking is poison to any civilization."

With the dawn of a new century, Webster not only wanted a healthier national climate politically, he hoped to turn people's attention to good health generally. He was flattered to be named a councilman in New Haven, and a justice of the peace as well. From 1800 until 1807, his neighbors and friends sent him to the state legislature.

"You could probably have a life in politics," Becca told him.

"It's too uncertain," Noah answered. "I will continue to write."

Write Noah did. For years he had put away information about the nature of diseases. What caused them? Where were they most likely to strike? What were the best treatments? Letters from doctors filled boxes and crates. Carefully, Noah took them out and pursued his study.

Slowly Noah plodded through his research. Most frustrating was the lack of good references—dictionaries, for instance, that offered a definition and example of a medical term. A doctor would refer to something that only he knew and understood. Nowhere could Webster find a mention of the term. Even Dr. Samuel Johnson's two-volume dictionaries offered few helps. In fact, they were filled with mistakes and omissions. There was not a mention of the United States or the Revolutionary War.

One afternoon, a red-faced Webster emerged from his writing room, carrying the two Johnson dictionaries, each one three inches thick and seventeen inches long. He hurled them to the floor, a sound which brought his wife running.

"What is it?" Becca gasped. "You look like you've been bitten by a snake!"

"Worse than that! I'm being driven mad by these worthless collections of nothing." Noah paused to gain his composure. "These books raise more questions than they answer!"

"But Dr. Johnson was considered a genius."

"A much over-rated reputation, I would say."

Becca smiled. "Perhaps he has provided more than frustration."

"And what is going on in that wily head of yours?" Noah asked.

"Only that once you complete your writing on epidemics and disease, you might compile your own dictionary."

"You and your foolish notions," Noah said, and laughed. He retreated into his writing room again, not bothering to retrieve the two books from the floor.

But Becca's thought did not leave him. In fact, it grew more and more attractive.

12

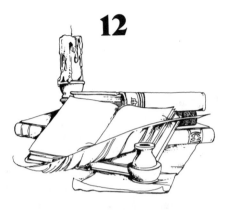

A New Century Begins

Noah sat back in his chair. He gazed solemnly at the water glass he held. Ordinarily, he would have been glad to welcome his old college classmate Joel Barlow to his home. But on this particular evening, early in 1800, Barlow brought news that troubled Noah. Even Becca was unable to brighten the conversation at dinner.

"And there were no leaders of the country there to represent us and other Americans?" Webster asked. "Our great general and president was put to rest without honor or recognition?"

"The mayor of Alexandria attended, and some other council officials," Barlow answered. "A local affair it was, with just a few members of his family, friends and neighbors in attendance."

Noah shook his head. It all seemed so wrong. As one century slipped into history, it took with it the most noble and prominent American. George Washington was gone.

News of Washington's death traveled at varying

speeds across the country. But always the reaction was the same. Shop owners, farmers, blacksmiths, craftsmen—all felt the loss. In New Haven, Noah felt he had lost a special friend.

"Tell me all you know of our great leader's final days," Webster said. "I need to know."

Carefully Barlow complied. On December 12, Washington had gone riding on his Mount Vernon estate, contracting a cold in the brisk winter winds. Summoned to tend the sick former President, physicians agreed that bleeding might confine the illness. In the study of illness and disease, Webster had already begun to have doubts about bleeding a patient. Washington steadily weakened, breathing his last shortly before dusk on December 14. His successor, John Adams, immediately ordered thirty days of official mourning.

"It just seems that more could have been done," Noah offered.

"Apparently, he was ready," Barlow replied, trying to comfort his friend. "It is said his final words were 'Doctor, I die hard, but I am not afraid to go'."

"I don't think our beloved leader was ever afraid of anything . . ."

"You could be right, Noah."

Ordinarily, a new century would have been greeted with happy celebrations, a hearty welcome. But Washington's death cast a gloomy pall over the nation. Noah seemed unable to cast away the depression he felt. He set aside his writing, turning instead to his gardening. Yet Becca could tell by the unenthusiastic manner with which Noah worked, that his mind was not on his efforts. Usually, he attacked weeds with a vengeance, carefully planting and culling young sprouts as if they were his children. Now he poked at the soil with his tools, his eyes often gazing up and looking away. Finally, Becca confronted him.

"Ever since we learned of General Washington's death, your thoughts have been elsewhere," she told him. "Death is inevitable, Noah. It comes to all men. . ."

For a long minute Webster said nothing. There was little indication he was listening. But when he eventually turned to speak, his eyes were filled with tears.

"Does it not seem terribly wrong to you that a man who led armies, who championed a nation, should go to his final resting place without any of the ceremony he has earned?" Noah stopped, his voice choking. "I remember him that night when I so boldly asked for his endorsement of my spellers. How wise he was, how kind. He taught me the importance of a man's name, his honor . . ."

"But Joel told us there was a local troop of soldiers to fire a final salute, and there were militiamen to escort the body. And he received the tribute due a great general, with his riderless horse following the procession."

Noah shook his head. "Oh, he deserved so much more than that. He had not even lived his three score and ten to which he was entitled. The grandest and most noble of all of us, and he is taken too early and with hardly a word of appreciation . . ."

So that was it. Words, Always words. A flush of anger colored Becca's cheeks. "Noah, when the Lord decides to call us home, it is our time. No matter how old we might be. You know that."

Noah was surprised at his wife. Seldom had she spoken with such force, such determination. He started to say something and then realized Becca was not finished.

"And as for words, they are not always necessary.

A great man has died, a good man. We are saddened by his loss because we respected and loved him. We feel that loss in our hearts. We do not have to express it in words. For my own part, I do not think I could. Perhaps you might be able to do so.''

Noah soaked in his wife's words, thoughts that undoubtedly she had harbored for some time. There was much wisdom in what she said. Setting the wooden hoe aside, Noah opened his arms wide. As Becca moved closer, Noah opened his mouth to speak. Lovingly, his wife reached a finger up to his lips.

''No words, husband of mine,'' Becca murmured, enjoying his closeness. ''Let our hearts speak silently.''

Noah nodded. He held his Becca closely, thanking God for sending her to him and whispering a final farewell to the man who had guided the nation in its earliest days.

As his depression eased, Noah again returned to his writing. In a sense, it was as if Washington's departure triggered a renewed interest in political affairs. He became a more frequent visitor in New Haven gatherings where local government issues were discussed. At times the air became hot with arguing. Noah enjoyed the heated temperatures, sharing his views with strong language and forceful gestures. Once more he was drawn into national affairs too, taking special exception to the actions of his former friend and business ally, Alexander Hamilton. ''This man who formerly seemed destined for greatness,'' Noah wrote, ''has seemed to cast all reason and honor aside. He does nothing but criticize President John Adams, yet offers few constructive thoughts himself. It would appear that venom has replaced ink in all of his inkwells.''

Hamilton was hardly deaf to Webster's comments. ''The man is a fool,'' he fired back in writing. ''He

would do well to turn his attention solely to his texts
for children. The events of the world are too difficult
for our dim-witted Webster to understand. Not only
that, he is too caught up in his own importance,
imaginary as that position may be.''

Tired of answering his attackers personally, Noah
brought his old friend *Prompter* back to life. In the past,
he had signed ''The Prompter'' to newspaper columns. To those who asked about this character,
Webster smiled. ''A Prompter is the man who in plays
sits behind the scenes, looks over the rehearser, and
with a moderate voice corrects him when wrong, or
assists his recollections when he forgets the next
sentence,'' Noah explained. The *Prompter* gave Noah
a chance to reach outside himself and offer comments
as an observer.

But Becca would not hear of Noah being totally
caught up in political activity and writing. Often she
would remind her husband of the need for a dictionary. To test the waters of public opinion, Noah
inserted a brief article in the New Haven newspapers.

> Mr. Webster of this city, we understand, is
> engaged in completing the system for the instruction
> of youth, which he began in the year 1783. He has
> in hand a *Dictionary of the American Language*, a work
> long since projected, but which other occupations
> have delayed till this time. The plan contemplated
> extends to a small Dictionary for schools, one for the
> counting-house, and a large one for men of science.
> The first is nearly ready for the press—the second
> and third will require the labor of some years.
>
> It is found that a work of this kind is absolutely
> necessary, on account of considerable differences
> between the American and English language, new
> circumstances, new modes of life, new laws, new
> ideas of various kinds give rise to new words, and
> have already made many material differences

between the language of England and America. Some new words are introduced in America, and many more significations are annexed to words, which it is necessary to explain. It is probable that the alterations in the tenures of land and ecclesiastical polity, will dismiss from the language in America several hundred words which belong in the English. The differences in the language of the two countries will continue to multiply, and render it necessary that we should have Dictionaries of the American language.

Most of Noah's friends and associates hailed his new project and wished him well. ''Your contributions to education and the quality of life are already substantial,'' wrote his friend James Madison. ''It is delightful to learn of forthcoming Webster projects.''

But the encouraging remarks were tempered by the usual negative comments. Noah's outspokenness about political affairs, as well as a rather over-confident demeanor, had brought him enemies and critics. One morning Webster opened his front door to find an envelope inside his front door. He opened it quickly. It was not a cheerful message.

My dear Master Webster,

The notification that you are once again embarked upon another literary project is sad news indeed. Why must you attempt to improve that which is superior to your own efforts? From our mother land England, we have the finest in literary presentations, including dictionaries. You only reflect your own inadequacies. Please spare us future offerings from the Webster pen. We shall be eternally grateful.

A Lover of Language

Twice Noah read the note. Then he crumpled the

piece of paper and headed toward his writing room. It was hardly the first criticism he had received, and he knew it would not be the last. As Becca passed her husband in the hallway, she looked into his face but she did not speak. She recognized the expression he wore—a look of anger and determination. Thoughts whirled in his mind, eager to jump from pen onto paper.

"This shall be the Prompter's task!" Noah exclaimed aloud as he plopped into his chair. Grateful his inkwell was full, eager Webster began to write.

An American Dictionary! Impossible! Who has the effrontery to attempt such a thing!

But perhaps some improvement can be made—

Improvement! What, improvement on Bailey, Johnson, Walker, Sheridan, Ash, Kenrick, and other English authors! Ridiculous! None but a blockhead would ever think of such a project! An American, a native of this God-forsaken country, where horses degenerate to palfreys, and man dwindles to a pigmy—an American harbor the audacious opinion that he can improve upon the words of British authors! I turn from the wretch with disgust and contempt!

But be quiet a little. Perhaps we have a few words not used in England.

Not used in England! Then banish them from the language. They are corruptions and must be rejected.

But suppose we have some new ideas, originating from new objects, new laws, new customs, new inventions; must we not use new words to express them?

New words! New ideas! What, Americans have *new* ideas! Why the man is mad!

But suppose this continent peopled with a hundred millions of inhabitants must they have no ideas, nor words, nor books, but what come from Great Britain?

Perhaps the British nation may hereafter learn something from America.

Pshaw! What nonsense. No, no. Keep to the authorities; never try to mend them. Let us have none of your improvements.

Satisfied he had answered his critics through the Prompter's imaginary conversation, Noah hurried to the New Haven newspapers. The editors were always glad for his contributions. Noah Webster was controversial, and controversy sold newspapers.

On his return home, Noah wore a wide smile. It always gave him a good feeling when he felt he had

written well. He glanced into the sewing room where he found Becca instructing their daughters with beginning knitting stitches. The woman glanced up, recognized the glee that sparkled in her husband's eyes, and smiled.

"Is this the same man I passed a few hours ago in the hallway?" Becca teased. "I think not, for that gentleman wore a frown with wrinkles of disgust lining his face.''

Noah nodded. ''It is indeed the same fellow, woman. But he has relieved himself with pen and ink since you last saw him. Words are always soothing to this brooding spirit.''

''Hm-m-m. And could this gentleman be the one Noah Webster of New Haven who is supposedly deep in work compiling dictionaries for the benefit of man?''

''Hold thy tongue, woman, or I shall list your name beside the word 'nag' in the dictionary I am writing.''

This time it was Becca's eyes that danced. ''I shall hold my tongue and be silent,'' she promised. ''But only if you take your pen and be productive.''

Turning from the doorway, Noah laughed. ''A worthy exchange, my dear wife. Let us begin at once.'' Whistling, a jovial Webster headed again down the hallway to his writing room.

13

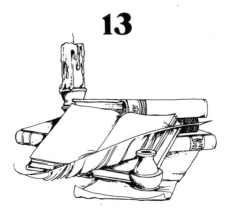

Climbing Mountains

"Compendious!"

Sitting back, Noah held the piece of paper up to catch the late afternoon sun. "Yes, compendious it shall be called. I only hope most people know that compendious means concise. Ah, well, if they don't, they shall after my dictionary finds their fingers."

Suddenly Noah stood up. In the distance he heard a child's cry. It was Julia. Her father was sure of it.

Leaving his study over the living room, Noah was directed by the cries toward the attic. The girls often played there, and sure enough, there sat nine-year-old Julia, two dolls locked firmly in her hands, staring out the window. Her crying had turned to deep sobs with tears making uneven paths down her cheeks.

"Is this my smiling Julia?" Noah asked at the doorway, his bushy eyebrows raised in exaggerated surprise. "No, no, it must be an intruder disguised as my second born."

The girl ran the back of her hand across her face, trying to rub away the tears. "Yes, Papa, it is I, Julia."

Noah crossed the room, smiling as he moved. He lifted his small daughter into his arms, then sat down with her securely in his lap. The ledge beside the dormer was filled with its two live occupants and Julia's dolls as well. "You know how I knew you really *were* my daughter Julia? Other girls your age would have said 'It is me, Julia.' And they would have been wrong. How proud I am of the fine way you speak. But to hear you cry saddens me deeply."

"I'm sorry, Papa. It was the boys at school. They were saying terrible things about you."

Noah kissed his daughter's forehead. "And what might they be saying that causes you to flood our house so?"

Julia looked into her father's face. Her eyes squinted in anger. "First, they said you had no business writing that book about epi-epi- well, you know."

"Epidemics?" Noah interjected.

"Yes, that one. And another boy said we're living in a traitor's house and only fools would do that. Are we, Papa? Did a traitor live in this house?"

Noah held his daughter closely. "Well, let's answer the first question first—should I have written a book about diseases, or epidemics? Well, some folks say I had no business writing such a book because I am not a physician. I say sour molasses to them. I'll write what I wish and they can read what they wish. I worked a long time on that book, eighteen months, and I took sick while I was writing it but I still finished. Most folks, including some fine physicians, think both volumes were a distinguished contribution to medical science."

"What about the traitor who lived here?" asked Julia.

"I'm afraid that's true. He was a general in the Revolutionary War named Benedict Arnold. He was a good soldier at first, but then he chose money over loyalty and love for America. He died last year in England, a sad, lonely man. But it does not matter that he lived in this house. That was a long time ago. What matters is that we live here now, and we are happy here. Is that not true?''

Julia hugged her father. "Oh, it *is* true enough. And I know what I shall tell the boys at school if they tease me further.''

"And what might that be?" Noah asked.

"Sour molasses!" Julia laughed loudly.

"A worthy retort!" her father replied. "Worthy enough to come from a Webster!"

The years spent in the former Benedict Arnold home in New Haven were productive years. Noah turned out writing about topics ranging from potatoes to animal history, and he was willing to speak freely to any local audience. As the stacks of Webster manuscripts grew, so too, did the Webster family. A fourth daughter was born, January 7, 1799, and named Mary. The fifth child and only son to live past infancy, William, appeared September 15, 1801. A fifth daugher, Eliza Steele, made her debut on December 21, 1805.

Although Noah spent most of the daylight hours at his writing table, he relished the strolls around town with Becca. Dressed often in black with a handsome long cane, the dapper Webster towered over the graceful, petite lady who was his wife as they walked beneath the rows of elm trees that dotted the city. Known to almost all of New Haven's 4000 inhabitants, the couple exchanged warm greetings and conversation willingly. What free time remained was spent in the garden where Noah enjoyed experimenting with mixed seeds and "newfangled" horticultural methods.

But no activity in New Haven consumed Noah's time and attention as did his work with dictionaries. For years he had jotted down new words, their pronunciations and meanings. His research on countless writing topics had turned up both simple and complex words. The 712 pages of the epidemic book produced over three hundred terms. Carefully, the diligent Webster alphabetized, updated, and pruned definitions. He wrote to experts in various professions and occupations, requesting additions and clarifications. He eliminated out-of-date offerings, but then would later put them back in.

"This is a more difficult battle than the Revolution!" he declared to Becca one afternoon.

"But you love it don't you?" she asked. Noah's smile, broad and beaming, was enough answer.

Webster's first dictionary, *The Compendious Dictionary*, was published in 1806. Some leftover political thoughts spilled into the preface, where Noah argued that America must be a self-reliant in language as she is non-entangled with foreign alliances. With the 408-page volume in his hands, Noah truly felt like a lexicographer or "dictionary maker."

"Now if people would but put my book to proper use," the proud compiler declared.

Becca smiled silently. Noting her expression, Noah asked for an explanation.

"It is nothing, husband of mine. Only that your remarks remind me of Luke 11:28—*'Blessed are they that hear the word of God, and keep it.'* Now we have the words of Webster."

Noah nodded. How often he had been accused of conceit. But never from his beloved Rebecca. He could see the teasing in her eyes and hear it in her voice. Well, two could play this game.

"I prefer I Corinthians 14:19—*'I had rather speak*

five words with my understanding, that by my voice I might teach others also, than ten thousand words in an unknown tongue.' Would you agree?''

Becca nodded. ''One truth is certain, my love. You will always have the final word, in your dictionary or out.''

Noah laughed.

But not everyone received *The Compendious Dictionary* so cheerfully. Some did not appreciate the criticisms of Samuel Johnson that Noah included in the book's preface. ''Word definitions are too long,'' remarked other authorities.

''I'll reduce the number of entries in the next edition,'' Webster promised, ''and I'll simplify some meanings. But my remarks about Dr. Johnson will remain.''

On November 20, 1806, a second son arrived at the Webster home. From the beginning, tiny Henry Bradford, fought for his life. The quill pen lay idle on the writing table as Noah stationed himself beside the infant's cradle. All that was known to be done was done, yet the child lived only nine weeks. ''The Lord gave, and the Lord hath taken away; blessed be the name of the Lord,'' Noah comforted his weeping wife.

To escape his grief, Noah buried himself in his work. He continued to explore the world of words, not only of the English language but others as well. The children squealed with laughter as their father shared his latest discoveries. He brought out his second dictionary in 1807, designed more for use in the schools. He had trimmed the first edition from 37,000 to 30,000 words. The price for the new volume was less, too, slipping from $1.50 to $1.00, and sales increased.

Like a bear hungry for a meal, Noah sought endorsements for his efforts. Politicians and educators offered enthusiastic testimonials. But no word came from President Thomas Jefferson. It was clear enough that Webster's earlier criticism had stung deeply.

In April of 1808, Noah again suffered personal tragedy. Louisa, born April 12, was found to be mentally retarded. It was a bitter blow, so soon after the death of baby Henry. Family and friends tried to comfort Noah, but he seemed deaf to their words. One well-meaning visitor overstepped his position.

"Surely you still do not hold to those beliefs in God," the man offered. "I, myself, have freed myself of such superstitions. You have believed and practiced your faith. How can you still believe in a God who would be so merciless?"

Noah stood at the window, gazing out. For a long moment, he said nothing. Finally, he turned. "Yes, I am hurting inside. Life can be painful. But without faith, without a loving trust in God, life would be impossible. It is God who sends us strength to endure hardship and heartbreak. He will remain in this house after all others have paid their respects and departed. He has always been with me, and I pray will be with me forever."

Slowly, step by step, Noah regained his desire to work. There were extra duties with Louisa, but each in the family accepted the responsibilities. It seemed to draw the parents and children even closer together. She was someone special, baby Louisa, who needed more love and help.

She was another mouth to feed, as well. No one realized that more than her father. He thrust himself into the greatest project of his life, a major American dictionary—a volume that would cause people to toss the outdated Johnson's model, and any other, aside. *An American Dictionary of the English Language* would combine the widest and most useful collection of any previous dictionary. It would be up-to-date, casting out the words of the past which never were used, and including those of the present which were. Recent medical terms would be there, words of business, geography, history and biology. Over the years, Noah had written about so many topics that he had a personal treasure-chest of entries in his own mind. Common words from other languages should be included, and words coined by major authors and politicians.

Certainly, it was a task that would take years. Although the royalties coming in from his Speller and Reader helped pay the bills, Noah charted a new means of raising money for the forthcoming dictionary. Whenever he could break away from his work, he traveled. Wherever he went, he enlisted subscribers—those who would put up ten dollars in advance for the new word volume. It was an odd arrangement, many thought, and the money did not flow in. He sought help from the government. Surely the United States itself, those leading the nation, would recognize the value of Webster's efforts.

"I am sorry to remark," wrote his friend Rufus King, "that I am able to discover but little probability of your receiving adequate encouragement to continue to devote your time and talents to the important and laborious investigation in which, for so many years, you have been engaged. Neither learning, morals, or wisdom seem any longer to be regarded as objects of public esteem and favour."

Not only did the government refuse to help with funds, Congress passed a law that hurt Webster further. A shipping embargo, pushed through by President Jefferson, drastically cut sales of Noah's books. With six children to support, the noted lexicographer looked for new means to earn money.

By 1811, Noah felt he had an answer. New Haven offered a certain warmth and liveliness, but it cost more to live there than in many other towns. At times, it seemed a bit too "lively"—especially for eleven-year-old William, who had acquired a few words not found in his father's dictionaries as well as an ability to fistfight with other unruly lads. When Noah was visiting in Amherst, Massachusetts, he discovered an imposing house on the east end of Phoenix Row. The ten acres accompanying the house would prove perfect for gardening and keeping orchards, additional avenues of saving money. A few questions revealed living in Amherst would be considerably cheaper than staying in New Haven, and Noah announced the Websters would be moving.

"Oh, must we!" exclaimed Emily, the oldest daughter.

"Can't we stay here?" begged the second oldest, Julia.

Noah glanced around the dinner table at the rest of the family. "I hear but two objections, a definite minority."

"But, Papa," Julia insisted further, "there are reasons we wish to stay here."

Emily nodded. "Personal reasons, Papa."

"And it is for personal reasons we must move," Noah declared. "If you consider eating and staying alive personal enough. Now if your personal reasons just happen to be William Ellsworth and Chauncey Goodrich, two fine young gentlemen with whom I sense you are a bit smitten, I have a notion such feelings will not dissolve whether you live in New Haven or Amherst."

Julia stood up, her mouth open in surprise. "Papa! How did you know?"

His eyes sparkling, Noah rubbed his chin. "I was

writing an entry for the word "love" this afternoon. I was pondering the use of you two young ladies with the two gentlemen I just mentioned. It would be an appropriate entry, don't you think?"

"Why, Papa!" Emily gasped, rising.

"Oh, you wouldn't dare—"

At the same time, both girls caught the teasing gleam in their father's eyes. They hurried to him, engulfing him with hugs and kisses. "It looks like we're off to Amherst!" he laughed.

14

Word Wizard

Slowly, Noah rose to his feet. He loved working in his garden, but now that he had slipped into his fifties, the body did not have the same oiled springs as it once did. He surveyed the immediate area, satisfied he had properly transplanted a hearty cluster of white grapevines from his father's supply in West Hartford. White grapes were unknown to the people around Amherst. It would be a special treat!

It was a wise move, from New Haven to Amherst, Noah was sure of that. The village of 1600 moved with a slower pace. Although William had not won an angel's reputation yet, neither had he shown signs of devilish behavior. Emily's and Julia's romances still seemed in full flower, and the rest of the children seemed to have fit in quickly. With her charm and warmth, Becca reached out to new neighbors and friends, entertaining them in the family parlor.

As for Noah, the changed quarters suited his purposes perfectly. As usual, he worked on his writing from early morning until four each afternoon. The

children walked on tiptoe past his study, never wanting
to disturb the master of the house. But the four o'clock
chimes meant an end to the day's labors. Cheerfully,
the children joined their father for conversation or
work in the garden.

The First Congregational Church in Amherst
proved a special magnet to the Webster brood. With
his three oldest daughters, Noah organized a church
choir. "Let your voices reach the Lord," Webster
encouraged his fellow singers. "And let Him hear no
discords." Once the choir was established, it seemed
only natural that a Sunday school be formed. By this
time, it was also natural for Noah to be the organizer.
But when he tried to get the Second Congregational
Church congregation to merge with the First Congregational Church congregation, the plan failed.
Gently Becca encouraged her husband back to his
writing.

Although Noah took a special interest in the War
of 1812, he stayed out of the political feuding as much
as possible. It troubled him to see the United States
fighting with other countries. He wanted the nation
to stay neutral and restrain from feuds of any kind.
Neighbors sought out his thoughts and opinions,
sending him to the Massachusetts legislature as their
representative. He refused to be drawn into the bicker-
ing of political parties, preferring a position on his
own. "You never know what Webster is going to say
and do," critics complained. But it did not change
Noah's behavior. He knew his own thoughts and
spoke his own mind. No pressure or criticisms would
alter that fact.

Like a bear in hibernation, Noah spent his time
recording by hand each word, each definition. His
reference books surrounded him in a semicircle and
he rolled on a coaster chair from source to source. Now

and then a human cry would come from the study, but Becca knew better than to intrude. It was just likely Noah had tumbled from his chair while excited about a new word discovery.

The years slipped by with few interruptions to Webster's work. Emily married her William, Julia her Chauncey, proving the move from New Haven to Amherst had been no obstacle to true love. Harriet, too, found a husband, and then Mary. But in 1819, while giving birth, Mary died. Her distraught husband could hardly function to care for himself, therefore Noah and Becca took the new infant in and adopted her as their own.

Only education pulled Noah from his writing. Wherever he went, his interest in local education remained strong. He was the guiding spirit behind the Amherst Academy which began in December of 1814 as a secondary school, and developed into a college seven years later with Webster as its president.

"You'll never complete your dictionary," scolded Becca, "if you allow yourself to be distracted. Learn to say no."

"Yes, my dear," Noah answered, staging a full bow. "I shall honor your words and return to my own."

Noah did more than return to his writing; he took his family back to New Haven. There were better library resources there. As his children married and moved out, expenses dropped. He could now afford life in his earlier community.

But Noah sensed there were still major gaps in his dictionary work. American libraries offered only so much. Across the ocean, European cities harbored giant treasures, shelves of reference books that seemed never to end. The mammoth libraries of Paris and London begged to be visited.

At the age of sixty-five, Noah Webster packed his bags. He did not want to make the long trip alone, therefore he persuaded William to come with him. Lazy and shiftless, the young man had done little to distinguish himself. Noah hoped to draw closer to his son, hoping to draw out "more of the Lord's goodness and less of the devil's doings."

Father and son set sail in June of 1824, immediately falling victim to sea-sickness. Cockfighting also turned Noah's stomach, but he enjoyed a competitive game of chess with any challenger.

With the arrival of the 4th of July, the ship's passengers celebrated with song, speeches and cheerful cheers. Noah shared tales of that Philadelphia some forty years before, when the Continental Congress signed the birth certificate of the new nation.

"We have come a long way since then," he declared, "and the future holds even greater promise. Let us toast the families and friends that we have, and pray that God will keep us all in His hands."

Settling in France, Noah soon felt he was in anyone *but* "God's hands." Prices for food and board were high, people were rude and abrupt, living conditions were unclean and distasteful. It was obvious the French cared little for American visitors.

But the treasures found in the major French libraries made up for the discomfort. Having spent so many years in his own writing room and the paltry library sources in America, Noah felt like a prospector striking gold. From each shelf poured rich nuggets— words and definitions never seen. Why, the Bibliotheque du Roi in Paris boasted 800,000 books and 80,000 manuscripts. "I could spend the rest of my life here," Noah told son William, "and believe I went to Heaven."

The sight of the determined lexicographer was a

familiar sight to many, as Webster prowled every spot
that might offer new selections for his dictionary.
Dressed in his usual black coat, black small-clothes and
black silk stockings, he was a human broomstick, his
slender, tall body poring over library tables. He put
in ten-hour days, making sure he had time to accompany William sightseeing in the evenings.

London, too, offered fine libraries. Cambridge

University, with 100,000 volumes, could not be
overlooked. While Noah rejoiced in word searching,
he was disappointed that at every opportunity, his
British hosts looked for a way to overcharge their
American visitors. But his letters home to Becca were
cheerful:

> *I have enjoyed very good health in Europe, & at no time
> for years past, have I been able to accomplish more business
> daily, than I have both in France & England. My indisposi-
> tions, from which I am rarely free, are slight and do not in-
> terrupt my studies. I have great cause of gratitude.*

Noah worked quickly. He hoped to complete his
dictionary by May of 1825. One day in January, as
he sat at his table in Cambridge, his hand started to
shake.

"Lord, please steady my pen . . ."

A moment later, Noah stood, He hurried to the window and threw it open. A brisk winter breeze snapped at the curtains as the tired notetaker breathed in deeply.

"I am finished," Webster sighed. "The task is done!"

It was a wonderful feeling for the sixty-seven-year-old gentleman from New England. At times, he had felt he might not live to see the end of his work. Now, he assembled the countless pages, the endless notes that related to his 70,000 word collection. How could he begin to thank his loving wife, his understanding children, his friends who had provided financial and moral support? Most of all, what thanks could he offer the ever-present God who shared direction and strength?

But in the midst of his joy, Noah encountered disappointment. He hoped to find a British publisher who could print the book at an inexpensive price and send it to America.

"Sorry, we have one of our own fellows putting together a dictionary," came one printer's reply.

Other printers and publishers stood by the work of Samuel Johnson. Why, it bordered on treason to consider putting out an American's dictionary!

"But mine has 12,000 more entries," Noah argued. "Johnson's is seventy years old and out of date."

No one seemed to listen. Sadly, Noah and William headed home. Having been gone almost a year, they received a glorious homecoming in New Haven. Everyone knew of the lexicographer's mission and cheered news of his successful completion. Noah was given the pin for Phi Beta Kappa, the elite organization for scholars. Yale, his alma mater, awarded him an honorary doctor of laws degree. He was welcomed into the Bunker Hill Monument Association, a select collection of patriots.

All the recognition was grand, but Noah was in a hurry to publish his dictionary. He dreaded the thought of again putting up his own money for the project. Could no one else see the value in his toil?

At last a man named Sherman Converse did. While the manuscript was set in type, Noah wrote advertisements. All modesty slipped into the wind like the fog. He was proud of what he had done. He criticized other dictionaries, claiming his own to be the greatest collection of words commonly in use, including legal, scientific and technological terms. His dictionary provided not only verbs, but verb participles. There were helpful and handy graphs and charts, and so much more!

"But it is the definitions that set my work a notch above the rest," Webster noted, "and that, after all, is what the quality of a dictionary depends on. There is a primary sense of every word, from which all others have proceeded; and whenever this can be discovered, this sense should stand first in order."

As pages rolled off the press, every word had to be checked and rechecked. It was a tedious and time-consuming task. Not until May of 1827 did the actual printing finally begin, on the presses of Hezekiah Howe, in New Haven. It was quickly determined that *An American Dictionary of the English Language* would not fit into one volume—two would be required, each numbering 1000 pages. Month after month slipped by, with Noah carefully supervising every step of the process. Then the pages had to be bound, the covers placed. It was November of 1828 before the first full sets were completed. The next cold morning found Noah bundling himself into warm clothes.

"And where might you be going on such a frosty day as this?" Becca asked.

"I'm going to deliver the first two dictionaries to

John Jay in Westchester County, New York. He has always stood by me, in fair winds or foul.''

Becca Webster smiled and shook her head. She knew it was hopeless to argue with her husband. At seventy years of age, Noah Webster would do as he pleased, whether it pleased anyone else or not. Arrogant? A bit, perhaps. But Becca felt he had reason to be proud. Becca watched her Noah ride off, and she felt all the love sweep through her, a love for a man who reached out to others and lived to serve.

An American Dictionary of the English Language won approval quickly. Members of Congress hailed the new volumes, calling them ''a better addition to the government than any one hundred laws.'' The judicial branch welcomed the books too, insisting that every courtroom should ''greet Webster willingly.'' Store owners discovered the dictionaries were grabbed up as soon as they arrived. Word games, according to Webster, were played in homes everywhere.

Sadly, publisher Converse had made other investments not as reliable as the fast-selling dictionaries. He was forced to declare bankruptcy, stopping the continued production of Webster's volumes. In order to pay the bills, Noah turned his attention to books of the past—earlier school texts and dictionaries that had been long neglected. He updated editions, adding and subtracting, according to the changing times.

But within Noah, there rumbled a wish to fulfill one final dream before he died. Most men in their seventies would have been glad to sit back, enjoy their children and grandchildren, and forget any major working enterprises. That was *most* men.

Noah Webster was different.

15

Confrontation

"Such foolishness, old man!" **Rebecca Webster**
stood at the doorway of their bedroom **watching Noah**
pack a trunk. "First you tell us you are ready to begin
an important writing project, and now you go running
off to Philadelphia."

"An observant wife would have noticed it has been
some time since her husband went 'running'
anywhere," Noah chuckled, tucking an extra
waistcoat neatly inside the rectangular box. "And a
loving wife would surely help her husband with a duty
such as this one."

Rebecca stepped forward, so accustomed she was
to helping her husband, but this time she retreated
instantly, folding her arms firmly in front of her. "No,
I'll not be helping you go and make a fool of yourself.
I would have thought you had better sense than this.
Why, those men in Philadelphia have criticized your
new dictionary just to test your temper. Why don't
you listen to the fine folks who say what a wonderful
thing you have done, that no one else could have done

it? Not you, Noah Webster! You listen to some sour windbags out West. I daresay they are baiting you the same way the devil baited Eve with the apple. Or has my loving husband been so long buried with his own book that he has forgotten the greatest Book of all?''

Noah closed the cover of the wooden trunk and carefully tied the rope straps around it. ''No, good woman, and you know better than that. God has blessed me with a gift and a love for words. I am now and always have been grateful for that kind blessing, Becca. Now I did not spend twenty-eight years of my life working on that dictionary to have men accuse me of doing it solely for money. From the very beginning, they have chosen to challenge my motives and my talents...''

''But they were poking fun at you because of your political views. Your critics have been almost all Democrats and because you share few of their political thoughts, you are a victim of their taunts.''

Noah nodded. ''That may be true enough. And many times have I turned the other cheek at their remarks, but this time I wish to answer them, if not for myself, for our children and our grandchildren. Now, if you wish to have me leave this house without a suitable parting, that is your choice. Otherwise, before I carry this trunk to the wagon, I would like to hold you in my arms before I depart.''

Becca shook her head slowly, as she did so often when she knew she lost an argument. Silently she moved forward, being swallowed up in Noah's embrace. ''Take care, old man,'' she whispered, ''and may the Lord bring you back to us soon...''

Noah smiled. ''I thought perhaps you were going to also ask Him to bring me back a wiser man.''

''Wisdom He has given you, with a hefty bit of

stubborness as well. Now, off with you.''

A few hours later, Noah was a passenger in a stagecoach heading west to Philadelphia. In the afternoon sunlight, he studied a crumpled, yellowed piece of newspaper copy he had pulled from a sheath of folders. Over twenty-five years before, the editorial had appeared in the *Aurora*, a Philadelphia periodical known to attack anyone supporting Federalist politics. Noah had been a target of pens dipped in venom before, but his public announcement in 1800 that he was undertaking an American Dictionary had brought about a biting announcement on the *Aurora* editorial page. When it had first appeared, Noah raged for days. Now, as he reread the article, he merely chuckled.

Noah Webster

There are some beings whose fate it seems to be to run counter from reason and propriety on all occasions. In every attempt which this oddity of literature has made, he appears not only to have made himself ridiculous, but to have rendered what he attempted to elucidate more obscure, and to injure or deface what he has intended to improve.

His spelling-book has done more injury in the common schools of the country than the genius of ignorance herself could have conceived of, by his ridiculous attempts to alter the syllable division of words and to new model the spelling by a capricious utterly incompetent attempt of his own weak conception.

After involving the question of the yellow fever in deeper obscurity and producing nothing but the profit by the sale of the work, he now appears as a legislator and a municipal magistrate of Connecticut; writes nonsense pseudo-political and pseudo-philosophical for his newspaper at New York, and proposes to give the American world no less than three dictionaries!

This man, who ought to go to school for the regulation of his understanding, has, it appears, undertaken to complete a system of education, and as a part of these, we are told, is to give us a dictionary for schools, a dictionary for the counting-house, and a dictionary for the learned.

His motives, for they are truly gothic, it appears, are that a number of British words have been misapplied—new words introduced—and a considerable number exploded in America; for this reason he says it is necessary to make a new Dictionary. The plain truth is, for the reason given is preposterous, that he means *to make money* by a scheme which ought to be and will be decountenanced by every man who admires the classic English writers, who has sense enough to see the confusion which must arise from such a silly project—and the incapacity of a man who undertakes a work which, if it were at all necessary or eligible, would require the labor of a number of learned and competent men to accomplish it.

"Indeed!" Noah muttered aloud, pondering how much more quickly the task might have been done with "a number of learned and competent men" working on it. His back suddenly tired, sitting on the coach seat he recalled the countless hours spent hovered over desks and tables, writing. How his hand ached from the hours of carrying words and definitions onto paper. In his mind, he galloped the horses faster along the road to Philadelphia.

From the moment he had learned that his new American Dictionary of the English language was to be the topic of an open discussion in one of the Philadelphia meeting houses, Noah had made plans to attend. Of course, he knew Becca was right. The messenger who had brought the news to their home hinted that it was a meeting called by those opposed to the recently published volumes. But what fun to attend, Noah thought. Hurry, horses, to Philadelphia, in haste!

Although Noah had friends in Philadelphia with whom he could have stayed, he chose instead to find rooms in an inn. After all, he wanted no embarrassment to fall on anyone he knew should the visit to the public meeting hall become some kind of incident. Anyway, he enjoyed being by himself now and then, a luxury seldom enjoyed at home. Years had vanished, and as Noah slowly walked the streets of Philadelphia, he remembered the excitement of 1787, when the Continental Congress was meeting. How honored he had felt when after only two days of meetings, General George Washington had called upon him in his rooms. And, of course, there was Benjamin Franklin, who loved words as much as Noah himself, and who had been assigned a guard to make sure the garrulous old statesman did not reveal any of the day's secret proceedings to those not attending. Both of the men were now long gone, but their voices still echoed in Noah's memory, and he felt their presence once again.

Before attending the public meeting, Noah hired a coach for a brief drive around the city. There was a freshness in the winter winds of 1828, perhaps an early hint of spring. How snug and proper the city sat along the Delaware River, with so many neat, red houses— Quaker homes—lining the streets. One could almost smell the delicious scrapple or cheesecake, or taste the fried oysters that adorned so many dinner table platters.

But more than the sights and smells of the city was its history. It was here that Andrew Bradford had published the first magazine on the continent back in

1741. The *American Magazine* it was called. And in
1783, the *Pennsylvania Evening Post and Daily Advertiser*
became the first daily newspaper in America. Yes, if
ever there was a city where words were important,
it was Philadelphia. The first magazine, the first daily
newspaper, not to mention the Declaration of Independence and the Constitution. Yes, Noah was glad
he had chosen to come here and speak in behalf of
his new dictionary. His beloved Becca might never
understand the reason for such a journey, nor would
the rest of his family. But good old Ben Franklin
might...yes, indeed, Ben would surely know what
Noah was doing in Philadelphia this March evening.

"We had better head to the meeting house," Noah
called out to the coach driver. "I would not want to
miss a moment."

By the time Noah reached his destination, the
meeting room was already half-filled. From a far
corner came the sounds of a harpsichord being played,
but the music was muffled by the sound of men talking. If the city air had seemed somewhat foggy outside, it was no match for the smoke that filled this
room. Noah chuckled to himself, slipping off his cloak,
wondering if he might have accidentally entered a convention hall for pipe smokers. Yet the murky air was
clear enough to reveal various clusters of gentlemen
in dark coats and pantaloons, silver shoe buckles
casting muted reflections in candlelight. Intentionally,
Noah skirted the outside of the area, hoping to pass
unrecognized in the quickly-filling chamber. But it
was not to be—

"Why, Master Webster," a voice hailed him from
several men away, causing those in between to turn
their heads in his direction. "This is indeed a surprise
and honor."

There was a tone in the greeting that caused Noah

to wonder whether it was a true statement. A "surprise" to find him in the gathering, perhaps, but hardly an "honor." Nonetheless, he accepted the hand that was thrust at his, carefully surveying the face now directly in front of his own.

"My name is Henry Jackson," the man said, bobbing a rather unkempt head of curly red hair. "It is good of you to come all the way from New Haven to defend yourself."

With a light smile, Noah shook his head. "That was not my purpose in coming, Sir. Unless, since I last visited this fair city, there has been a law passed against creative scholarship. In that case, I have no defense."

"Ah, you shall pick at my every word..."

"Words are my business and my love," Noah declared. "I choose each one as I choose a friend, with caution and care. But I will confess that the topic of your evening *has* drawn me here this evening. I would have thought I might have received an invitation, yet none arrived by messanger or post. Perhaps it was an oversight..."

"Well, ah, yes, perhaps that might have been a thought to be considered." Master Henry Jackson was clearly a bit flustered, as conscious of the men who were watching the brief exchange as he was of the quickness of Noah Webster's thinking. "If you will come forward, I shall seat you at the table in the front of the room. Some may have questions, and you may wish to offer your de-de... explanations.

Noah nodded. "It shall be my privilege and I thank you for the opportunity."

Voices lowered as Noah followed Master Jackson to the front of the room. The kerosene chandeliers were turned up by an attendant, revealing the immense cloud of smoke that covered the room. Few of those holding pipes made any effort to douse their instruments, but instead crowded closer to the front for a better view.

Seating himself at the table, Noah hoped that his attire befitted such an occasion. Most in the room had not come to heap compliments and praise, of that he was certain, but he did not want to be an object of their scorn because of a yellowed shirtcloth or a stained coat or trouser. For a moment his mind recaptured the times long ago when he spoke to such gatherings about the importance of a strong educational program in the country. On such a night he might have welcomed such a crowd as this one, at least in number. But as he heard the muffled undertones and sensed the sneering glances, he prayed a silent prayer for strength and clearness of thought.

Master Jackson wasted little time with introduction; Noah was simply labeled "the dictionary man from New Haven" and told to explain his actions. Slowly the seventy-year old man rose, smiled at his audience, and then gazed down. "I have never been in a court-room on trial," he offered, "but this, I believe, comes as close to that experience as I should like to come. Perhaps I might explain how I came to produce the two volumes which have gathered your attention..."

Hearing no disapproval, Noah continued. He recalled the day, some twenty-eight years ago, when he had first set out on the mission. To that point in time, the most accepted dictionary was that of Dr. Samuel Johnson—two large books of some fifty thousand words that had taken the noted British gentleman some eight years to complete.

"But sadly enough," Noah continued, his voice gaining in strength as he spoke, "there were many mistakes, many omissions. Errors in providing the history of words from foreign languages, and words

left out because the book was published in 1755, before many of us were born. Pages were wasted with the rambling quotations of long forgotten authors, information no longer useful for people living today.''

From across the table, Henry Jackson leaned forward. ''And you felt that *you* were the one, self-appointed, to provide us with a better dictionary. Might I ask how many foreign languages you have learned. Might I further ask if you are aware that your own publication contains errors?''

''I shall answer your first question by saying that I arranged my work area in a giant semi-circle, my chair on wheels so as to trace quickly a word in the reference books resting on tables before me. The languages I used? English, of course, Russian, French, Spanish, Italian, Greek, Latin, Swedish, Danish, Dutch, Armoric, German, Anglo-Saxon, Irish, Persian, Hebrew, Ethioptic, Samaritan, Arabic, Chaldaic, Syriac, and a few dialects.''

Audible murmurs could be heard in the crowd, clearly reflecting that Noah had made quite a positive impression with his recitation. The feeling gave him confidence.

''Now, as to errors,'' the lexicographer went on, ''I am certain there are many, some created by the machines which produced the final dictionary and the others donated by this humble servant who stands before you.''

''Yet as you dare to criticize Dr. Johnson for mistakes, then you admit to making mistakes yourself!'' Henry Jackson looked to the group. ''A humble servant, this man calls himself, but I think he imagines himself considerably more. I think he fancies himself touched by God Almighty, come to cure the ills and pains of this world. He does not like the books in our schools, so he throws them out and writes his own. He does not like the way our leaders carry out their public offices, so he writes to newspapers and shares his own views. He does not like the way others have handed down our language, so he provides his own wares.'' Back to face Noah, Henry Jackson turned, his lip curled in disgust. ''I think, my friend, you are a worthless critic who seeks only to line his pocket with all the money he can.''

This time Noah did not look down. He gazed at his accuser. ''You are wrong, Sir, deathly wrong. I am merely a man who has traveled the road of life, trying to follow God's direction, and serving those around me and beyond. As to lining my pockets, I have probably invested more money into my publications than I have ever taken from them. I have spoken out and written where I felt there was a need.''

''Was there a need, Sir, to take a language, finely honed, and relegate it downward by use of modern slang and sub-standard usage?''

''If you mean, Master Jackson, to include those words and phrases that are American rather than pure English, yes, I believe there was such a need. No one would wish our people to speak and write with accuracy more than I do, but a dictionary's purpose is to share meanings with *all* the people. I have included no words or definitions that our general citizenry would find offensive for it is my notion that good breeding casts out such usage. No, to my thinking, the dictionary is a schoolbook, a text that any child might consult with definite purpose or for pleasure.''

''Perhaps replacing the Bible?'' Jackson countered.

Noah's eyes sparked, his jaw jutting defiantly forward. ''Never, Sir. Even the thought is outrageous. The Bible guides our souls, our spirits. My offering merely offers help for what we say and how we say it.''

"But why you?" one of the men nearby asked. "No one has elected you to anything, yet you feel compelled to speak out on how we handle our affairs with other countries. You are no physician, yet you write a book about diseases. As I understand it, you failed as a schoolmaster, yet you write books on what our children should learn. Who has given you the right?"

Noah glanced over at Henry Jackson, who had seated himself comfortably, letting a colleague take on the battle. There was a long pause.

"It would seem a bit strange, my friend, that you of Philadelphia would need reminding from a visitor from New Haven regarding the rights and freedoms of any citizen of this country." Deliberately, Noah surveyed the room. "You all seem of noble purpose, of reasonable understanding. Surely we have not forgotten what took place in this very city some fifty years ago. Did not some brave men assemble here to carve out a Declaration of Independence, and later still, a Constitution, that would preserve for all of us certain rights, certain freedoms?" Noah turned back to his questioner. "Who has preserved my right? Why, Washington did, and John Hancock, and your precious Benjamin Franklin. Not only did they preserve it for me, they preserved the same rights for you. Should you wish to pen a book, do so. If it not be libelous or treasonous, it shall be printed and read. Indeed, it may be criticized, but more importantly, it is your right."

Henry Jackson rose. "Let me ask you you, Master Webster, whether or not your first thought upon completing your-your dictionary was to wonder how much money you might earn through this collection of words and meanings?"

Noah smiled. "Sir, I remember the moment well last October 16th, when I had finished the final proof sheet for the dictionary. It was my birthday, you see, and it was with such a goal that I had hoped to finish this long effort and send the books along for assembling. Wiping the ink from the quill, I set it down and capped the inkwell. I removed my spectacles...at the age of seventy, Master Jackson, you may succumb to such devices...and I gazed across the desk at my wife Rebecca. She, too, had endured the twenty-eight years of tedious work. Without speaking, for even I have learned there are moments when words play no part, we took each other's hands and knelt together in prayer. We gave thanks to God for His providence in sustaining us through the long labor of this effort. And now, I believe I will excuse myself so that I might make plans to return to that woman and my family in New Haven. I must confess she thought me a bit foolish to come here, but I have no regrets. You have given me an opportunity to speak and I am grateful. You may discuss my dictionary, criticize it, tear out its pages, do what you will. For what errors it contains, I apologize. For the fact that it exists, I am proud. Thank you, gentlemen.''

Noah made his way through the crowd, not looking into any of their faces. As he reached the doorway, he thought he heard a pattering of rain on the roof. But no, it was not rain at all. It was clapping. Yes, the people behind him were applauding, and it grew louder and louder. For a brief moment, Noah turned and smiled. Then he slipped into his cloak and hurried into the night.

16

A Final Mission

Noah Webster had a secret.

"You say he still goes into his writing room each day from eight until four o'clock?" Julia asked her mother one day as they visited.

Becca nodded. "With but a short time for lunch."

"And he gives no clue as to what he's writing?" daughter Emily inquired.

"None at all. Whenever I ask, he merely smiles. 'You shall know soon enough, my honeybee', he answers."

Julia slowly shook her head. "That certainly does not sound like Papa."

"No, indeed," Emily agreed.

Yes, Noah's secret caused many questions to be raised. Spellers, readers, grammars, articles, public letters, dictionaries—each one he was writing, he announced for the world what he was doing. Even after the giant dictionary was finished and he had turned to updating his earlier works, everyone knew what he was doing.

But now he was again hibernating in his writing

room, day after day, week after week. What could he be working on? One point was certain—no one was willing to trespass into those inner chambers. The writing room belonged to Noah and no one else. It was as if a NO TRESPASSING sign was posted on the door.

How Noah relished the mystery he created. At family gatherings, he enjoyed those who would try to make him reveal his secret.

"I'm planning to visit Boston next week," son William offered. "Perhaps I might pick up some books you could use in your work."

"A kind and thoughtful gesture that would be," his father answered, "but not one I'll be needing."

"Perhaps I might help you script," daughter Harriet suggested. "Surely your eyes tire as you work. You always have told me how fine my penmanship is."

Noah lifted his hand to scratch his head, a head whose grey hairs now outnumbered the darker shades of his younger years. "Another gracious offer," he declared. "Becca, we are blessed indeed with grand helpers. But I think that you should save your penmanship, Harriet, perhaps to post some letters to our family and friends."

As the months slipped away, Noah could not contain his excitement over his writing activities. When he revealed he was preparing his version of the King James Bible, some family members were apprehensive. After all, Noah was no minister and had no advanced schooling in theology. It did not bother the famed lexicographer. "I have been criticized before," he noted. "I have studied Hebrew, Greek and Latin on my own. I shall do my best. Personally, in this task, I am more interested in serving my Master than the people around me."

First, Noah tackled the older uses of words contained in the King James Bible. *Who* replaced *which*, in reference to people. All his life, Noah had disliked the recited "*Our Father which art in heaven . . .*" The use of *who* provided a warmth, a sensitive feel. Previously, the First Psalm had read: 3. *And he shall be like a tree. . .that bringeth forth his fruit in his season, his leaf also shall not wither, and whatsoever he doeth, shall prosper.* When Noah finished his work on the First Psalm, it read: 3. *And he shall be like a tree. . .that bringeth forth its fruit in season; its leaf also shall not wither; and whatever he doeth shall prosper.*

Obsolete words were tossed out as Noah substituted new terms. Why use *three score* when *sixty* could be used? Was there a reason to say *gather together* in place of *assemble*? Webster did not think so.

And finally, Noah gave way to his own feelings about the use of Biblical language he felt "violated decorum" or proper breeding. He replaced "breast" with "bosom," and he used "limb" rather than "leg." Such changes clearly reflected his personal modesty.

The first King James Bible with Noah's alterations appeared in October of 1833. In spite of the years he had spent on the work, Webster refused any royalties. "It is hardly a work I can claim as my own," he stated. "I have only attempted to repair a few problems. I hope my efforts prove fruitful. To have completed this mission is to have toiled in the vineyard of the Lord."

Noah's version of the King James Bible met with mixed responses. As anticipated, there were those who felt that only a theologian should have attempted such a task. Other critics missed the beauty of the old language that Noah had replaced with more modern usage. The strongest criticism came from those who felt Noah's personal changes to make the book cleaner or "more modest" were absurd. "Why would this Webster fellow squirm at the use of a word like 'leg' and not be repulsed by the ugly degradation and sin of the book's villains?" asked one minister.

The harsh words hurt. At seventy-five, Webster hoped that he had shared his greatest contribution. Yet there came few commendations. Two years after the revision was published, in 1835, Noah felt crushed. "I wish a few clergymen would summon courage to commend my Bible to the public. It wounds my feelings to observe how indifferent the people are, and especially clergymen, to the correction of words which are somewhat difficult to understand in the common version."

Despite the lack of approval, Noah was glad he had undertaken the task. To a friend, he wrote that the experience had given him a " partnership with God." In a handbook written to accompany his revision of the King James Bible, Noah supported his feelings of faith:

> ". . . We find the true religion of Christ in the Bible only. It is a scheme wonderfully simple, the principles of which are all comprehended in two short phrases, love to God and love to men. Supreme love to God, the source and model of all excellence, is the foundation of the whole system of Christianity; and from this principle in the heart flow all the benevolent affections and exercises which constitute piety. The persons who love God supremely will reverence His character and laws, and will extend his benevolent affections and charities to all his creatures. From this source will proceed love to man, and the careful performance of all moral and social duties."

From here and there came a few statements backing Noah's efforts. The instructors at Yale University, standing loyally behind their graduate of long ago, issued their support and approval. That was somewhat gratifying, yet it was less than Noah would have liked, or hoped.

Noah, as always, didn't find much joy in the political affairs of the nation. Although he had tried to devote himself to his writing and stay uninvolved with politics, his disgust with President Andrew Jackson could not be hidden. In his mind, Noah felt Jackson was little less than a dictator, wanting more and more personal power. But Webster worried too, about the people of the nation. He felt they could be too easily led, too swayed by men of words. And who would know better about the power that men with words could have than Noah Webster himself?

Once again, the aging lexicographer inked his quill pen and began writing letters to newspapers. This time he used the name Sidney, not wanting anyone to judge his thoughts because of who he was. He wanted his ideas evaluated on their content alone. Offering warnings and advice, he spoke to the people and their elected leaders, urging care and caution as they made decisions. "There is good and bad in all men," Noah wrote, "and all too often the devil can make his voice sweet and honeyed. Weaker men can be misled, believing they are following the road of honor and good. Beware, those who would be taken along such a pathway, for you are waiting prey for those who would use you."

But for all practical purposes, Noah considered his literary career complete. He had given his beloved country a body of quality literature, proper in grammar and broad in content. Through his books, young people learned spelling, writing, manners and patriotism. He had shown the people new ways of understanding their country, its culture and government, its strengths and weaknesses. He had angered some, informed many and delighted readers throughout the nation. He had given them language, organized and defined their own words, and shown them how to use them. He had brought the Holy Scripture into the modern world, tightened it, clarified it—and, perhaps, wrapped it in his own prejudices.

To the Webster home in New Haven came people of all ages, of all professions, men and women alike. Noah received his guests in the front sitting room. He sat in a high-backed armchair where he could gaze into a constant fire in the fireplace. Across the room sat Becca, sewing and mending in a rocking chair, seldom speaking but forever attentive to her husband's needs.

As Noah slipped quietly into his eighties, he became even more mellow. Two daily trips to the local post office brought him outside, as did occasional afternoon strolls with a visiting grandchild. He was known to all those who passed by. Many enjoyed a moment's conversation with him before moving along. Now and then he spoke excitedly on a topic, but for the most part, his voice was sure and steady, his manner reserved.

Noah and Becca observed their fiftieth wedding anniversary in October of 1839. No celebration was held because all family members could not be present. "With anyone of them missing, it would be meaningless," Noah declared. "There will be another time."

But at 81, time was running out for Noah. Would he be able to enjoy a final family gathering? He hoped that he would, and as usual, he prayed for such an opportunity.

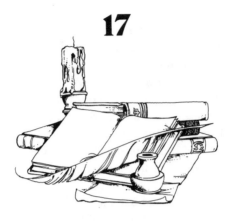

Sunset

Noah looked at himself in the mirror. He straightened his vestcoat, hoping to press away a bit of the bulge which had found a home around his middle. "Becca's fault!" he chuckled to himself, remembering the extra cherry tarts she always saved for him.

"Are you ready?" His wife's cheerful voice sang into their bedroom chamber from some other spot in the house. No doubt she was cleaning or straightening or tidying something—that was her way. "William is bringing the carriage around soon."

"In a moment or two," Noah shouted back. He ran a comb through a shock of grey hair which had once been a light auburn, a mite displeased that it no longer lay spread evenly as it once did. Ah, well, there was a healthy supply of it at least, and for a man of eighty-three, that was blessing enough.

It was a special day, and yet it was an ordinary day as well. Daughter Julia had organized the Webster family to officially observe the fiftieth wedding anniversary of Noah and Rebecca.

"A rather silly notion," Noah scoffed, "seeing that such a date occurred some two or three years ago."

Julia would not be put off. "And have *you* never missed a deadline, Papa? Have you never planned to have a manuscript complete at one time and found yourself early or late?"

"My, I have raised a saucy young lass!" he laughed, pleased with his daughter's quick retort. "Fair enough. We shall celebrate our anniversary in May rather than October. It would seem the ladies of the world carry a louder and louder voice. Now years ago—"

But before Noah could finish, his audience disappeared. So often he recalled "years ago," and most of his family had heard the stories many times. Oh, the stories of meeting General Washington, of dining with Benjamin Franklin, of being a college boy at Yale—those tales carried a special interest. But so often the tales carried a long moral, a sermon of sorts, and for that, the Webster relations preferred their own clergymen.

On May 4, 1842, the Webster clan celebrated and honored their beloved patriarch and matriarch in an anniversary observance. The Julia (Webster) Goodrich parlor was where sons and daughters, grandsons and granddaughters, great grandsons and granddaughters, and a few extra kin thrown in "just for fun," all gathered. With joy in their hearts and tears in their eyes, the gathering filled the air with the strains of "Auld Lang Syne" and "Home, Sweet Home."

The singing completed in the front parlor, the family headed to the back parlor where tables were decked in flowers and food. Smells of roast pig, venison and turkey filled the air, mingling with aromas of freshly-baked pies. Noah and Becca were seated in the middle of the assembly, in guest-of-honor positions. Chauncey Goodrich, son-in-law of the anniversary couple, asked that heads be bowed for prayer.

"We are grateful indeed to gather together in love and thanksgiving," offered the host. "We have been blessed by the presence of our own beloved Noah and Rebecca for many years, and they have enjoyed fifty—"

Noah coughed a trifle, gaining his son-in-law's attention.

"—over fifty years of wedded bliss. On this day, we thank You, Lord, for this food, these people, and Your love. Amen."

Immediately knives and forks attacked the sumptuous banquet—the men slicing hefty pieces of meat, mothers cutting food into baby portions for infants in the group, and laughter filling the air. Later, as Becca excused herself, Noah leaned close.

"Are you going to let the corset out a bit to make room for dessert?" he teased.

His wife flushed, and brushed him off with a "Hush yourself, old man," and scurried away.

Appetites satisfied, again the bulk of the group returned to the front parlor, leaving a troop of female soldiers to cart away the plates and complete their duties in the kitchen. Noah reigned supreme among those gathered for storytelling. Tales of a long-ago youth floated back and lived once more. Never had his family shown him such attention. Finally, he leaned from his chair and asked a six-year-old great-grandchild, "What makes you so quiet today, Arthur? You don't usually sit without a fidget."

The boy looked up, his face filled with honesty. "I was told to be respect-respect . . . good or I'd get a switchin' when I got home."

A few in the group exchanged worried looks. But Noah eased their worries.

"An honest lad who speaks the truth!" The old man laughed. "We should have more of the same! Truly a Webster!"

From the Goodrich home, the well-fed and cheerful entourage headed to the home of the honored guests for sweet tarts and tea. This time it was Becca's turn to preside, pouring from polished silver heirlooms and showing off her baking skills. The stories continued, growing more imaginative with the passing hours. Finally, it was time to part. But before anyone left, Noah gathered his family in prayer.

"May God in heaven choose to bless us all here, and those who follow us in future generations. Here, as we share the warmth and richness of each other's love, let us not forget the Savior who looks upon us all. Let us, by our every word and action, carry His message to all we meet."

Rising to his feet, Noah embraced every person present—the young children as well as all the adults. No one left empty-handed. Each carried a new Bible, the Webster edition, of course, with a ribbon tied around it.

That anniversary party was remembered over and over by Noah and Becca. Memories of the past replaced activities of the present.

However with encouragement and coaxing from friends, Noah got busy and put together a collection of essays entitled *A Collection of Papers on Political, Literary and Moral Subjects*. The volume went to press in April of 1843.

The spirited step of the past was gone now. Garden tools were set aside in the backyard tool shed. Noah continued his daily walks to the post office, but his trips to visit relatives and friends dwindled.

The church bells of New Haven tolled loud and
clear on the morning of Sunday, May 21, 1843. It
had been a moody spring, never able to make up its
mind whether to be warm or cold. Noah dressed
lightly for the day, hoping to give an early welcome
to summer.

"You might wear a heavier cape," Becca
cautioned. "The wind has a chill to it."

Noah shook his head and smiled. "More of a hearty
bite to it, is all. I shall be fine."

Noah spent the entire day at church, enjoying the
sermon and remaining for the afternoon prayer
services and socializing. It was dusk by the time he
returned home, and he had a slight shiver.

By Tuesday, the shiver had turned worse. By the
end of the week, his illness had become pleurisy, and,
it was so serious there seemed to be little hope for his
survival. Family members were summoned. How
weak Noah seemed, how pale and tired!

Becca maintained a faithful vigil. She would not
leave her husband's bedside. "He might want a drink
of water," she explained, as if there was a need to
account for her actions.

By Sunday, May 28, 1843, Noah was conscious one
moment and unconscious the next. Voices from the
past returned, and scenes from his life. The end was
near.

"I'm ready to go," he whispered. "My work is all
done. I know in whom I have believed. I have
struggled with many difficulties. Some I have been
able to overcome, and by some I have been overcome.
I have made many mistakes, but I love my country,
and have labored for the youth of my country, and
I trust no precept of mine has taught any dear youth
to sin."

With loved ones nearby, shortly before eight o'clock

in the evening, Noah Webster, Jr. died.

Across the nation, newspapers carried word of the death of the noted lexicographer. President John Tyler said, ''The nation has lost one of its most illustrious citizens. Noah Webster played a vital role in the initial formation of this government, the education of its youth, and the strength of the nation's fabric. America is in his debt.''

Funeral services were held at the Center Church in New Haven, while memorial services were conducted at Amherst College. ''He was a man of God who spent his life serving people,'' the church gathering was told. ''He was born to a Christian family, lived the Christian faith and died in the Christian faith. Noah Webster will be no stranger to God.''

The Grove Street Cemetery around the corner from his home in New Haven provided Noah's final earthly resting place. Four years later, Rebecca joined him.

EPILOGUE

"Look it up in Webster."

How many boys and girls have been given that suggestion? It is impossible to know. Yet it is a fact that when any American thinks about dictionaries, the name Webster comes quickly to mind.

During his lifetime, Noah Webster worried much about money. Although his efforts to protect his own literary works earned him the title "father of the American copyright," the royalties he received barely paid his debts. Often he found himself financing his own writings. But after his death in 1843, Noah Webster's heirs enjoyed the rewards of his efforts.

G.&C. Merriam Company of Springfield, Massachusetts contacted Chauncy Goodrich, Noah's son-in-law, and asked him to enlarge the *American Dictionary of the English Language*. It came out as a one-volume edition in 1847, sold for six dollars, and when the copyright was renewed, paid the Webster family $250,000.

Illustrations first appeared in the dictionary in the 1859 edition. Five years later, Noah Porter edited *Webster's Unabridged Dictionary*. Porter again revised the book in 1890, and it immediately found a place among the 300 million English-speaking people in the world.

With the 1900s, and the expiration of the original copyright, many publishers began issuing "Webster dictionaries," some aimed at specific audiences such as college and high school students. Over fifty books presently listed in the annual volume *Books in Print* carry the Webster name. It is obvious that publishers recognize the quality and prestige suggested in the Webster name.

The Webster version of the King James Bible did not enjoy the immediate acceptance and approval as did his dictionary, speller and other texts. Naturally, anyone, especially a one-man, self-appointed, reviser of the King James Bible opened himself to criticism. But there is little doubt that Webster's updating of vocabulary and reshaping of phrases made the Book more easily understood for countless Americans. Published in 1833, it was as if Noah Webster had spent a lifetime working with language so that he could finally attempt this "most important enterprise," his version of the King James Bible. His magnificent effort lives on in reprints today, finding its way into the hands, hearts and minds of people everywhere.

"What a man does with his life may or may not be remembered after he is gone," Webster observed. "That does not matter. What matters is that a man's actions are worthy in the eyes of God and useful to his fellow man. I pray my life has been of worth and usefulness."

Was the life of Noah Webster "worthy in the eyes of God" and "useful to his fellow man"? Perhaps the pages of this book suggest an answer.

BIBLIOGRAPHY

Ford, Emily Ellsworth Fowler, *Notes on the Life of Noah Webster* Emily Ellsworth Ford Skeel, ed. 2 volumes, (New York: privately printed, 1912; reprinted 1971 by Burt Franklin, New York)

Higgins, Helen Boyd, *Noah Webster-Boy of Words* (Indianapolis: Bobbs-Merrill Company, Inc. 1961)

Morgan, John S., *Noah Webster* (New York: Mason/Charter, 1975)

Proudfit, Isabel, *Noah Webster* (New York: Julian Messner, Inc. 1942)

Rollins, Richard M., *The Long Journey of Noah Webster* (Philadelphia: University of Pennsylvania Press, 1980)

Scudder, Horace E., *Noah Webster* American Men of Letters Series, edited by Charles Dudley Warner (Boston: Houghton Mifflin Company, 1882)

Shoemaker, Ervin C., *Noah Webster, Pioneer of Learning* (New York: Columbia University Press, 1980)

Warfel, Henry Redclay, *Noah Webster, Schoolmaster to America* (New York: The Macmillan Company, 1936)

INDEX

ABOUT THE AUTHOR

David Collins—teacher, author, speaker, a man of many talents—lives in Moline, Illinois. He has written at least forty-five books and is still going strong. Other Sower Series books from his typewriter are *Abraham Lincoln, George Washington Carver, Francis Scott Key, Florence Nightingale,* and *Johnny Appleseed.*

Mr. Collins has been honored by many organizations, including the Junior Literary Guild, the National Book Council, and the Illinois Council of Parents and Teachers.

"When I write for young readers," says Mr. Collins, "I attempt to apply a 'double E' standard to my work. I hope to *entertain* and *educate.* I want my young readers to enjoy the experience of reading and take something away from it too, even if it's just one new word or one different idea."

ABOUT THE ARTIST

Michael L. Denman says he has always liked to draw. He remembers that in his poor family paper was scarce. So his grandmother gave him her Christmas cards, which in those days were always folded into fourths. Michael unfolded them and was delighted to have full sheets of paper, blank on one side, ready for his drawings. His favorite books as a child were those on history, so he especially likes to illustrate history books for today's children. He reads each book before illustrating it and his children read it too. They enjoy talking together about the history books.

Mr. Denman at first learned most of his art skills by himself, but later he studied art at Cooper Institute. For more than ten years he has illustrated children's storybooks, workbooks, and readers, as well as visual aids that teachers use. He is an Art Director at McCallum Design Company and lives with his wife and family in North Ridgeville, Ohio.

SOWERS SERIES

* New title coming soon